GLOSSARY OF PLANT PATHOLOGY

Editors

Mr. R. Naveenkumar
Department of Mycology and Plant Pathology, Institute of Agricultural Sciences,
Banaras Hindu University, Varanasi, Uttar Pradesh, India

Dr. S. R. Prabhukarthikeyan
Scientist (Plant Pathology), Crop Protection Division, National Rice Research
Institute, Cuttack, Odisha, India

Mrs. U. Keerthana
Scientist (Plant Pathology), Crop Protection Division, National Rice Research
Institute, Cuttack, Odisha, India

Published by

JPS Scientific Publications
India

Published by

JPS Scientific Publications, Tamil Nadu, India.
E.mail: jpsscientificpublications@gmail.com
Website: www.jpsscientificpublications.com

Published in India.

International Standard Book Number (ISBN): 978-81-946500-1-0

JPS Scientific Publications also publishes its books in a variety of Electronic formats. Some content that appears in print may not be available in Electronic formats. For more information visit our publication website www.jpsscientificpublications.com

ISSN: 978-81-946500-1-0

PREFACE

This book would be much useful to the readers to know the terminologies in the field of plant pathology particularly to the beginners. The attempt was made to cover in details of various terminologies in the area of mycology, plant bacteriology, plant virology, epidemiology, host pathogen interaction and applied aspects of plant pathology. This book would be assist the students of undergraduate plant virology, plant pathology, microbiology, botany and post graduate students in plant pathology, botany with the specialization of plant pathology, microbiology. Also the book glossary of plant pathology could be helpful for the students who is preparing for various competitive examination such as ICAR-JRF, SRF, NET, entrance exams for various SAU's, CAU'S and BHU (PET). There would be acontinuous effort on the part of the authors to revise, update and modify the contents of the book. Theauthors are deeply thankful to individuals, who helped on time for successful preparation of this book.

Mr. R. Naveenkumar

Dr. S. R. Prabhukarthikeyan

Mrs. U. Keerthana

ABOUT THE BOOK EDITORS

Mr. Naveenkumar R, is currently doing Ph.D in Plant Pathology, Department of Mycology and Plant Pathology, Institute of Agricultural Sciences, Banaras Hindu University, Varanasi, Uttar Pradesh. He has completed his B.Sc. (Agriculture) and M.Sc. (Agriculture) from Faculty of Agriculture, Annamalai University, Annamalai Nagar, during 2013 and 2015, respectively. He is the recipient of UGC research fellowship in his Ph.D program. He has qualified ICAR-NET examination during 2016. He also served as senior research fellow in ICAR-NRRI, Cuttack, Odisha during 2016. He has participated in many national and international conferences, seminars and workshops and presented papers across the country. To his credit he has published more than fifteen research papers in national and international journals, five book chapter and eight popular articles.

Dr. Prabhukarthikeyan S R., graduated in agricultural science and earned his Master's and Doctoral degrees in the field of Plant Pathology from Tamil Nadu Agricultural University (TNAU), Coimbatore. He has joined as Scientist (Plant Pathology) at Indian Council of Agricultural Research on July, 2015. He is having good experience in molecular basis of host-pathogen-bioagent interactions, induced systemic resistance (ISR) and proteomics. He has published thirty research papers in peer reviewed journal and has authored fifteen popular articles, one book, ten book chapters. He is in the review panel of peer reviewed journals. He received many certificate of appreciation in recognition of his review work from International Journals.

Mrs. Keerthana U., graduated in agricultural science and earned his Masterdegree in the field of Plant Pathology from Tamil Nadu Agricultural University (TNAU), Coimbatore. She has joined as Scientist (Plant Pathology) at Indian Council of Agricultural Research onJan, 2015. She has published twenty research papers in peer reviewed journal and has authored ten popular articles andfour book chapters. She has good experience in biological control of fungal diseases and molecular techniques of plant pathology. She is in the review panel of peer reviewed journals.

- **A**biotic: Nonliving, or caused by a nonliving agent; e.g., abiotic disease.

- **Accessibility:** cellular conditioning toward pseudosymbiotic relation induced by compatible pathogens.

- **Accession:** taxonomic classifier for host plants below the species level. Accessions refer to individuals of a plant population that were collected from specific geographic regions and often have different NB-LRR protein arsenals. Differential growth of individuals of a pathogen species then serves to define different strains /isolates/races of a given pathogen species.

- **Accessory pathogens:** support keystone pathogens in their establishment in the community by nutritional or colonization support and find their niche in the pathobiome.

- **Acervulus:** A flat or saucer shaped fruiting body with a stromatic mat of hyphae producing conidia on short conidiophores. An acervulus lacks a definite wall structure and not having an ostiole or definite line of dehiscence

(or)

Acervulus: Most of the fungi belonging to the order melonconiales of the deuteromycotina sub division produces acervuli. It is nothing but a saucer shaped depressed mass of aggregated hyphae bearing conidiophore in a compact layer on its exposed surface. In between the conidiophore, long pointed dark coloured structures called *setae* are present. On the host, acervuli are initially developed below the cuticle or epidermis and become erumpent on maturity. (eg) *Colletotrichum* sp., *Pestalotia* sp.

- **Acquired resistance:** a resistance response developed by a normally susceptible host following a predisposing treatment, such as inoculation with a virus, fungus, bacterium, or treatment with certain chemicals. This resistance is not inherited.

- **Acquisition access period (AAP):** the period of time given for the vector to acquire the virus.

- **Acquisition feeding time:** the feeding time during which a vector feeds on an infected plant to acquire a virus for subsequent transmission (e.g. to become viruliferous).

- **Action threshold:** the soil population density of nematodes at which some action should be taken to limit both yield losses and population density increases.

- **Acylalanines:** The acylalanines are also referred as phenyl amides, acylanilides and acylanilines.

- **Adeno Virus:** Any of a group of spherical DNA viruses characterized by a shell containing 252 capsomeres, infecting number of mammalian species including man; some are oncogenic.

- **Adenosine:** A ribonucleoside containing purine adenine.

- **Aerobe:** An organism which grows in the presence of oxygen

- **Aflatoxin:** A mycotoxin produced by the fungus *Aspergillusflavus*and by some other fungi.

- **Agar:** A gelatin-like material obtained from seaweed and used to prepare culture media on which microorganisms are grown and studied.

- **Agglutination:**a term used in serology to describe an antibody-antigen reaction in which large clumps of reactants are involved, as when antibodies are attached to latex particles before mixing with the virus antigen.

- **Agro-ecosystem:** the ecosystem that develops on farmed land and which includes both the crop species and its associated microorganisms and the indigenous microorganisms, plants, and animals.

- **Agroterrorism:** Thedeliberate introduction of an animal or plant disease with the goal of generating

fear over the safety of food, causing economic losses, and/or undermining social stability.

- **Allele:** One of a pair or series of alternative forms of genes that occur at a given locus in a chromosome.

- **Allopatric speciation:** the formation of two or more species from a single ancestral species following geographical isolation of subpopulations.

- **Alteration of generations:** The regularly occurring alternation of haploid (gametophyte) and diploid (Saprophyte) phases in the life cycle of sexually reproducing plants.

- **Alternate hosts (Wild hosts of other families):** The role of alternate hosts is not as important as of collateral hosts. However, when a pathogen has very wide host range (as *Sclerotiumrolfsii, Rhizoctoniasolani, Fusariummoniliforme*etc.) and is tolerant to wide range of weather conditions the alternate hosts become very important source of survival of the pathogen. These alternate hosts are very important for the completion of the life cycle of heteroecious rust pathogens.

- **Alternate Splicing:** Widespread mechanism by which a single gene can encode two or more proteins.

- **Ambidextrous activator:** one that simultaneously contacts more than one target site on RNA polymerase.

- **Ambimobile**: When chemical moves in both the directions (having both acropetal and basipetal transport) **Eg.**: Systhane, Imazalil, Fosetyl – AL

- **Amino acid:** Any one of the class of organic compounds containing the amino (NH_2) group and the carboxyl (COOH) group; the building blocks of proteins.

- **Aminopurine:** The base analogue producing transitions.

- **Amphipathic:** an amphipathic peptide contains both polar and nonpolar domains.

- **Amplification:** Creation of many copies of a segment of DNA by PCR / Duplication of genes within a chromosomal segment

(or)

Amplifications: The production of additional copies of a chromosomal sequence found as intrachromosomal or extrachromosomal DNA.

- **Anaerobe:** An organism which grows in the absence of oxygen

- **Analog:** a sequence derivative of a given peptide.

- **Anamorph:** asexual ("imperfect") form of an ascomyceteor basidiomycete fungal pathogen (characterized by the presence of conidia).

- **Anastomosis:** The important cause for heterokaryosis is anastomosis. Anastomosis involves fusion of hyphae of some species, movement of one or more nuclei into one or the other of the fused cells, and the establishment of a compatible heterokaryotic state.

- **Angstrom unit (A°):** A unit of length equal to one ten thousandth of a micron (10^{-4} micron; a micron being 10^{-6} meter), also equivalent to 10^{-1} millimicrons (mμ) or 10^{-10} meter; named in honour of the Swedish physicist Anders Jones Angstorm

- **Anisogamy:** If both gametes are motile but dissimilar

- **Annealing:** A laboratory technique by which single strands of DNA or RNA having complementary base sequence become paired, to form a double stranded molecule.

- **Antheridium:** Male gametangium is called as antheridium. Male gametangium is small and club shaped

- **Antibiosis**: Antagonism mediated by specific or non-specific metabolites of microbial origin, by lytic agents, enzymes, volatile compounds or other toxic substances is known as antibiosis.

(or)

Antibiosis: The antibiotic compounds secreted by the

biocontrol agent suppress the growth of the pathogen.

- **Antibiotics**: Antibiotics are generally considered to be organic compounds of low molecular weight produced by microbes. At low concentrations, antibiotics are deleterious to the growth or metabolic activities of other micro-organisms.

- **Antibody:** a protein which is produced in the body in response to foreign substances such as bacteria or viruses.

  (or)

  Antibody: a specific protein formed in the blood of warm-blooded animals in response to the injection of a protein or polysaccharide.

- **Antifungal:** referring to a substance which kills or controls fungi.

- **Antigen:** a protein or polysaccharide which induces the formation of antibodies when injected into a warm-blooded animal. The capacity of an antigen to react specifically with an antibody is referred to as *antigenic reactivity.*

  (or)

  Antigen: a substance in the body which makes the body produces antibodies to attack it, e.g. a virus or germ.

- **Antimicrobial:** referring to something which is capable of killing or inhibiting the growthof microorganisms, especially bacteria, fungi or viruses

- **Antioxidant:** a substance which prevents oxidation, used to prevent materials such as rubber from deteriorating and added to processed food to prevent oil going bad.

- **Antiseptic:** preventing or reducing the growth of harmful microorganisms.

- **Antiserum:** a serum taken from an animal which has developed antibodies to bacteria and formerly used to give temporary immunity to a disease.

  (or)

- **Antiserum:** The blood serum containing antibodies possessed by a warm-blooded animal.

- **Antisporulant:** A chemical inhibit spore production without affecting vegetative growth of fungus. e.g.: Bordeaux mixture, Metal containing fungicides.

(or)

Antisporulant: The chemical which inhibits spore production without affecting vegetative growth of the fungus.

- **Antitoxin:** an antibody produced by the body to counteract a poison in the body.

- **Aplanospores**: Sporangiospores which are non motilewithout flagella are called aplanospores.Eg. *Rhizopusstolonifer, Mucor*

- **Apoplastic movement**: When compounds move in the direction of transpiration stream through the xylem vessels (It is upward movement). **Ex**: Benomyl, Carbendazim,Carboxin,Oxycarboxin, Kitazin, Tridemorph.

- **Apothecium:**
Ascocarpproducesasci in open.

(or)

Apothecium: It is an open cup shaped ascocarp with a wall peridium. The asci are arranged in a layer called hymenium, either exposed from the beginning or later exposed

- **Appresorium**: Flattened tip of hyphae or germ tube acting as pressing organ by attaching to the host surface and gives rise to a minute infection peg which usually grows and penetrates the

(or)

Appressorium: an infection structure formed by rust fungi on the leaf surface, generally over stomata.

(or)

Appressorium: The swollen tip of a hypha or germ tube that facilitates attachment and penetration of the host by a fungus.

- **Arbuscule:** A branched, tuft-like haustorium, produced by certain mycorrhizal fungi inside root cells.

- **Area under the disease progress curve (AUDPC):** The area of a graph under the line that depicts the progress of an epidemic.

- **Argonaute (Ago):** proteins family that constitutes RNA silencing effector and is characterized by a small dsRNA RNA-binding domain, PAZ and a slicer domain, PIWI.

- **Armadillo repeat:** a 42-amino acid "arm"motif repeat first identified in the Drosophila segment polarity gene product armadillo (β-catenin).

- **Ascocarps:** Ascocarps are the fruiting bodies of members of Sub-division Ascomycotina which produce the asci containing the ascospores.

- **Ascomycotina:** Thallus is septate mycelium. Rarely unicellular. Motile spores are absent. Asexual spores are conidia.Sexual spores are ascospores produced endogenously in an ascus.Sexual reproduction mainly by gametangial contact.

- **Ascospore:**Sexual spore produced in a specialized sac like structure known as ascus. Generally 8 ascospores are formed

- **Ascostromata**: The asci are formed directly in cavities called locules with in stroma. The stroma itself serves as wall of ascostroma. Sterile structures called pseudoparaphyses are present in ascostromata.

- **Aseptate hypha/coenocytic hypha:** A hypha without septa is called aseptate /non-septate/ coenocytic hypha wherein the nuclei are embedded in cytoplasm.

- **Attainable yield:** a reflection of a given production situation; the yield performance of a crop that has not been exposed to yield-reducing factors, especially pests.

- **Attenuated strains:** pathogenic microorganisms, mainly bacteria and viruses, which have lost their virulence.

- **Attenuation:** Partial or complete loss of virulence in a pathogen.
- **Autoclave:** It is an apparatus in which saturated steam under pressure affects sterilization called autoclaving. The pressure increases boiling point of water and produces steam with a high temperature. Cells are destroyed by high temp and not by the pressure. Most of the organisms are killed at 121 °C and 151b pressure per sq. inch in 15 min.
- **Autoecious fungus:** A parasitic fungus that can complete its entire life cycle on the same host.
- **Autoecious rust:** If all the spore stages are produced on the same host then the fungus is called autoecious and the phenomenon is called autoecism.
- **Auxotroph:** A strain which lacks the ability to synthesis one or more essential growth factors.
- **Avirulence:** The inability of a pathogen to infect a certain plant variety that carries genetic resistance.
- **Avoidance**: Avoiding disease by planting at times when, or in areas where, inoculum is ineffective due to environmental conditions, or is rare or absent.
- *Avr*gene: pathogen gene that elicits specific resistance in its host plants with a corresponding *R* Gene.
- **Avr protein:** The protein coded for by an *Avr*gene, acting as an elicitor of defense reactions.
- **AVRx:** microbial avirulence factor matching resistance gene X.
- *Azotobacter*: a nitrogen-fixing bacterium belonging to a group found in soil.

- **B**acteria: very small organisms, invisible except through a microscope, belonging to a large group, some of which help in the decomposition of organic matter, some of which are permanently in the intestines of animals and can break down food tissue and some of which cause disease.

- **Bacterial attachment site:** The DNA base sequence in bacterium at which a prophage is inserted

- **Bacteriocins:** Bactericidal substances produced by certain strains of bacteria and are active against some other strains of the same or closely related species

- **Bacteriophage:** a virus that affects bacteria (or) a group of viruses that requires bacteria as host cells

- **Bacteriostatic:** Capable of inhibiting bacterial growth without killing them

- **Basal body:** Small granule which a cilium or flagellum is attached

- **Basal resistance:** immunity that still occurs in susceptible interactions, does not protect the plant, but restricts pathogen's virulence.

(or)

Basal resistance: race-nonspecific host resistance that is active in susceptible plants and limits the severity of disease.

- **Base pair change:** Any change in a base pair in DNA

- **Base pair mismatch:** The presence of a hetero-duplex region in double stranded DNA

- **Base pair ratio:** A+T/G+C ratio

- **Base pair substitution:** A class of lesions in DNA molecule, which may give rise to gene mutation where purine may be substituted by another purine (transition) or by a pyrimidine (transversion)

- **Base pair:** A pair of bases (A-T or G-C) one in each strand that occur opposite one another in a double stranded DNA or RNA

- **Basidiomycotina:** Thallus is septate mycelium.Motile spores are absent.Clamp connections and dolipore septum are present.Sexual spores are basidiospores produced exogenously on basidium.Sexual reproduction is by spermatization and somatogamy.

- **Basidiospore:** Sexual spore produced on a club shaped structure known as basidium.Generally 4 basidiospores are formed. Eg, *Puccinia*

- **Beaker:** It is a simple container for stirring, mixing, and heating liquids. Commonly used in many laboratories. Beakers are generally cylindrical in shape, with a flat bottom. The traditional use of a beaker is to hold liquids.

- **Biflagellate zoospore:** A zoospore with two flagella, situated laterally or anteriorly on zoospore.

- **Bifurcation:** sudden change in long-term behavior of system in response to small change in parameter value.

- **Binary fission:** An amitotic asexual division process by which a parent cell splits transversely into daughter cells of approximately equal size.

- **Bioassay:** The use of a test organism to measure the relative infectivity of a pathogen or toxicity of a substance.

- **Biodiversity:** the range of species, subspecies or communities in a specific habitat such as a rainforest or a meadow. Also called **biological diversity.**

- **Biofilm:** A polysaccharide matrix in which one or more species of bacteria and fungi are embedded. May play a role in bacterial and fungal attachment, colonization, and host invasion.

- **Biological association:** a group of organisms living together in a large area, forming a stable community.

- **Biological control:** the control of pests by using predators and natural processes to remove them.

(or)

Biological control: The reduction of inoculum density or disease producing activity of a pathogen or a parasite in its active or dormant state by one or more organisms accomplished naturally or through manipulation of the environment of host or antagonist by mass introduction of one or more antagonists (Baker and Cook, 1974).

- **Biological oxygen demand:** ameasure of the amount of pollution inwater, shown by the amount of oxygen needed to oxidize the polluting substances.

- **Biopesticide:** a pesticide produced from biological sources such as plant toxins that occur naturally.

- **Bioremediation:** the use of organisms such as bacteria to remove environmental pollutants from soil, water or gases (NOTE: Bioremediation is used to clean up contaminated land and oil spills.)

- **Biosecurity:** the management of the risks to animal, plant and human health posed by pests and diseases.

- **Biotechnology**: It is defined as genetic modification and manipulation of living organisms through the novel technologies such as tissue culture and genetic engineering resulting in production of improved or new organisms that can be used in variety of ways.

- **Bioterrorism:** The frightening and terrorizing of civilian populations by terrorists spreading or threatening to spread microorganisms pathogenic to humans in ways that can reach and infect the people.

- **Biotic:** Living; associated with or caused by a living organism.

- **Biotroph:** An organism that can live and multiply only on another living organism. They always obtain their food from living tissues on which they complete their life cycle. Ex: Rust, smut and powdery mildew fungi

- **Bipolar mating system:** incompatibility system with one locus that has two (biallelic) or multiple(multiallelic) alleles.

- **Bitunicateascus**: The ascus wall consists of 2 layers.At the time of spore release,the exotunica bursts and the endotunica expands up to twice or more of its original length separating from exotunica while exotunica remains as originally formed. The spores are released through a pore at the tip of endotunica.In this,the walls are separated. The behavior of bitunicateascus during discharge of spores is described as Jack- in a box.

- **Blight:** sudden death of twigs, foliage, and/or flowers.

- **Blotch:** large and irregular-shaped spots or blots on leaves, shoots, and stems.

- **BOD (Biological Oxygen Demand) incubator:** It maintains a range of temperature below and above the optimum levels (5 to 50°C) require for the growth and multiplication of microorganism. The incubator is provided with both heating and cooling system.

- **Boot:** stage follows emergence of the flag leaf collar and continues until the spike begins to emerge.

- **Bordeaux mixture:** a mixture of copper sulphate, lime and water, used to spray on plants toprevent infection by fungi.

- **Bordeaux Mixture:** This fungicide was introduced by Professor Millardet of University of Bordeaux, France in the year 1882 for the control of downy mildew disease of grape vine. It is prepared by using the ingredients copper sulphate, quick lime and water in the proportion of 5:5:500.

- **Bordeaux Paste:** It is a preparatory copper fungicide and it consists of same ingredients as that of Bordeaux mixture but in the form of a paste. The paste is prepared by adding 5 kg each of copper sulphate and lime in 50 litres of water. It is basically a wound dressing fungicide to be applied to pruned parts of host plants such as ornamental plants (Rose) and fruit crops (Ber, citrus and grapes etc.) to prevent fungal attacks.

- **Broadcast:** In this method fungicides are mixed with soil or fertilizers, and scattered with hand as uniformly as possible over the field and mixed with the soil with a

suitable implement. This method involves greater quantity of fungicides than other methods.

- **Budding:** The spores formed through budding are called blastospores. The parent cell puts out initially a small outgrowth called bud / blastosie.,sprout or out growth which increases in size and nucleus divides, one daughter nucleus accompanied by a portion of cytoplasm migrates into bud and the other nucleus remains in the parent cell. Later, the bud increases in size and a constriction is formed at the base of bud, cutting off completely from parent cell. Bud, when separated from parent cell, can function as an independent propagating unit.Sometimes multiple buds are also seen i.e., bud over bud and looks like pseudomycelium.

- **Bunsen Burner:** It is a piece of lab equipment that is used to heat materials for experiment. It is a burner which operates on gas. The flame of a burner can be adjusted by managing the inflow, outflow and mixing of gas and air. A Bunsen burner is named after the inventor Robert Bunsen a scientist working for the University of Heidelberg in 1855.

- **C**anker: dead places on bark and cortex of twigs or stems; often discolored and raised or sunken.

- **Capsid:** a protein coat/shell that encloses and protects the virus genomic RNA/DNA.

  (or)

  Capsid: The protein coat of viruses forming the closed shell or tube that contains nucleic acid.

- **Capsomere:** The morphological sub-units seen on the surface of the virus particle (virion) in the electron microscope. A capsomere is built up from varying numbers of protein sub-units (polypeptide chains).

- **Capsule:** A relatively thick layer of mucopolysaccharides that surrounds some kinds of bacteria.

(or)

Capsule: Sharply defined layers present external to bacterial cell

- **Capture probe:** the sequence-specific fragment of DNA bound to the solid support in a microarray.

- **Cartagena Protocol:** The Cartagena Protocol on Biosafety is an international agreement on biosafety, as a supplement to the Convention on Biological Diversity.

- **Cavity slide:** It is a concave glass slide which is used for assessing spore germination assays particularly those pathogens they produce spores.

- **Cell wall apposition:** cell wall material deposited at sites of microbial attack that differs in chemical and mechanical features from the normal cell wall.

- **Cell wall:** A rigid structure secreted external to the plasma membrane containing cellulose and lignin in plants

- **Center of origin:** the geographical place of origin of a species.

- **Centrifugation:** the separation of the components of a liquid in a centrifuge.

- **Centrifuge:** It is an apparatus that rotates at high speed and separate substances or particles on the basis of mass and density by means of centrifugal force. The centrifugal force is noticed in rpm (revolutions per minute). It consist of a head which is rapidly revolved by an operate motor. Generally 4 metal cups or containers are attached to the head for holding tubes. The particles get settled at the bottom of the tubes.

- **Certified seed:** seed which has been successfully tested for purity, disease and weed contamination and is granted certification for sale.

- **Chemical food poisoning:** poisoning by chemical substances in food, e.g. by toxic substances naturally present in some plants or insecticides in processed food.

- **Chemigation:** In this method, the fungicides are directly mixed in the

irrigation water. It is normally adopted using sprinkler or drip irrigation system.

- **Chemotaxanomy:** Chemotaxonomy is the study of chemical variations in living organisms, and the use of these chemical characteristics for classification and identification.

- **Chemotroph:** an organism which converts the energy found in organic chemical compounds into more complex energy, without using sunlight.

- **Chitin:** A complex, N-containing carbohydrate, derived from *N*-acetyl-d-glucosamine, forming the hard outer shell of insects, crustaceans, arthropods, fungi, and some algae.

- **Chitinases:** enzymes that cleave poly-β-1,4-N-acetyl-glucosamine (chitin)

- **Chlamydospore:** A thick-walled asexual spore formed by the modification of a cell of a fungus hypha.

(or)

Chlamydospores: Chlamydospore (Gr. *Chlamys*= mantle + *spora*= seed, spore) is a thick-walled thallic conidium that generally function as a resting spore. Terminal or intercalary segments or mycelium may become packed with food reserves and develop thick walls. The walls may be colourless or pigmented with dark melanin pigment.

- **Chlorosis:** yellowing of normally green tissue due to reduced chlorophyll content, such tissue is *chlorotic.*

- **Circulative transmission:** viruses circulate into their vectors bodies before their transmission.

- **Circulative viruses:** viruses that move from the gut into the hemolymph and other tissues of their vectors.

- **Clamp connection:** Clamp connection is a mechanism found in Basidiomycetes. It is a bridge-like hyphal connection characteristic of

the secondary mycelium in many Basidiomycetes. In ensure that sister nuclei arising from conjugate division of the dikaryon become separated into two daughter cells. Clamp connections are found during nuclear division and supposed to help in dikaryotization of adjacent cells.

(or)

Clamp connections: It is a hook like structure formed laterally in between the dividing nuclei in a dikaryotic hypha. It acts as a by-pass for the nuclei, as they cannot pass through septal pore ie.,dolipore septum. It is meant for multiplication of dikaryotic cells.

- **Cleistothecium:** Asci are produced in completely closed ascocarp

(or)

Cleistothecium: It is a completely closed ball like (globose) ascocarp and it is made up of a wall with pseudo-parenchymatous tissue called as peridium. In some species these are provided with outer

appendages. Asci are scattered or distributed at different levels in ascocarp.When the asci are matured, ascospores are released by disintegration of peridium.

- **Cloning:** The term used to express the construction of recombinant DNA molecules

- **CNL:** CC-NB-LRR protein, an R protein containing a central NB-ARC domain fused to an N-terminal non-TIR domain and a C-terminal LRR domain.

- **Coalescent theory:** a retrospective population genetic model based on genealogies of the alleles of a gene. It uses statistical analyses to infer the coalescence of lineages back in time to the most recent common ancestor (TMRCA).

- **Coat protein:** the protein unit, typically, but not always, of one type, that makes up the virion capsid.

- **Coexistence:** simultaneous occurrence of two species without one of them being excluded by the other.

- **Cold treatment:** the use of freezing to disinfest storage containers.

- **Collateral hosts / Alternative hosts (wild hosts of same families)**: Collateral hosts are those which are susceptible to the plant pathogens of crop plants and provide adequate facilities for their growth and reproduction of these pathogens during offseason. Weeds which survive and live during non-cropping season provide for the continuous growth and multiplication of the pathogen. Thus the weed hosts help to bridge the gap between two crop seasons.

- **Colonization:** A successful infection requires the establishment of a parasitic relationship between the pathogen and the host, once the host has gained entry to the plant.

  (or)

  Colonization: establishment of pathogen population within a field or production region.

- **Colony counter:** It is an electronic apparatus used to count the number of colonies on a Petri plate.

- **Commensal microorganism:** organism living on exudates and nutrients provided by the plant host without having a negative effect on the host.

- **Commensalism:** symbiotic relationship that is beneficial to one organism and neutral to the other.

- **Competition:** The biocontrol bacteria and fungi compete for food and essential elements with the pathogen thereby displacing and suppressing the growth of pathogen.

- **Competitive disease model:** viruses usurp a substantial amount of host resources to cause disease.

- **Competitive exclusion:** competition between species that is so intense that one of the species entirely eliminates the other species.

- **Complementary DNA (cDNA):** DNA synthesized by reverse transcriptase from an RNA template.

- **Composting:** the controlled decomposition of organic waste, especially used for the disposal for plant waste in gardens or domestic green waste such as vegetable peelings.

- **Conical flask:** An Erlen Meyer flask, also known as a conical flask, it is widely used type of laboratory flask which features a flat bottom, a conical body and a cylindrical neck, it is named after the German chemist Emil Erlen Meyer who created it in 1860. Erlenmeyer's are also used in plant pathology for the preparation of microbial culture medium.

- **Conidia / Conidiospores:** Conidia are non- motile asexual spores which may arise directly from somatic hyphae or from specialized conidiogenous cells (a cell from which conidia are produced) or on conidiophore (hypha which bear conidia)

  (or)

- **Conidia:** Conidia are the asexual spores produced by most of the higher fungi (*terrestrial fungi*) including ascomycotina, basidiomycotina and deuteromycotina.

- **Conidiophore:** A specialized hypha on which one or more conidia are produced.

- **Conjugation:** Transfer of the genetic material from one cell to another through cell contact (Mating)

  (or)

  Conjugation: Union of sex cells or unicellular organism during fertilization, a one way transfer of genetic material from a donar to a recipient

- **Conks:** fungal fruiting structures formed on rotting woody plants (shelf or bracket fungi).

- **Consequential virus-host interactions:** interactions that directly contribute to the establishment of a systemic infection.

- **Consortia:** Groups of cells formed by stable mixed species

- **Contamination of soil:** Contamination of the soil takes place by gradual spread of the pathogen from an infested area to a new area or by introduction of contaminated soil, plant debris to a new area or by introduction of infected seed or planting materials.

- **Continuous resistance:**a response involving a gradient from severe infection to extreme resistance in a segregating population.

- **Cork borer:** It is used to punch holes on an agar plate to perform well diffusion assays. Often used in a chemistry or biology laboratory is a metal tool for cutting a hole in a cork or rubber stopper to insert glass tubing

- **Co-speciation:** concerted speciation of a host and its pathogen. The reproductive isolation and subsequent speciation (sexual incompatibility) of hosts drives the concomitant reproductive isolation and speciation (sexual incompatibility) of the pathogen.

- **Coupled translation or coupled termination/ re-initiation:** a translation mechanism allowing some portion of ribosomes to translate the downstream ORF after they terminate the preceding ORF of single polycistronic mRNA.

- **Crop loss (damage):** any decrease in quantity (yield loss) and/or quality of a crop output; damage may lead to loss. Note that crop loss encompasses yield loss.

- **Crop sanitation:** Collection and destruction of plant debris from soil will help in the management of soil borne facultative saprophytes as most of these survive in plant debris. Collection and destruction of plant debris is an important method to reduce the primary inoculum.

- **Cross protection:** The phenomenon in which plant tissues

infected with mild strain of a virus are protected from infection by other severe strains of the same virus. This strategy is used in the management of severe strains of *Citrus Tristezavirus*

- **Cross-talk:** the induction of population density-dependent responses in cells of one bacterial strain or species by acyl-HSLs secreted by another strain or species.

- **Cryo-transmission electron microscopy:** transmission electron microscopy of unstained, unfixed, frozen-hydrated (vitrified) specimens, preserved as close as possible to their native state.

- **Culture:** To artificially grow microorganisms or plant tissue on a prepared food material; a colony of microorganisms or plant cells artificially maintained on such food material.

- **Curative fungicide**: a fungicide that is applied to plants once they have been infected with a fungus rather than as a preventative measure.

- **Cyanobacteia:** These are large and heterogenous group of phototrophic bacteria. They oxygenic and related to gram positive bacteria.

- **Cyst:** the bodily remains of a dead female cyst nematode.

Damping-off: destruction of seeds in the soil, or seedlings near the soil line, resulting in reduced stand, or the seedling falling over on the ground

- **Dauer:** from the German for enduring, describes an alternative life cycle stage that enables nematodes to survive adverse environmental conditions.

- **Decay:** a process by which tissues become rotten and decompose, caused by the action of microorganisms and oxygen to rot or decompose

- **Decline:** progressive, gradual weakening and death of a plant or population of plants

- **Decompose:** to break down into simple chemical compounds by the action of sunlight, water or bacteria and fungi.

- **Decomposition:** the process of breaking down in to simple chemical compounds

- **Defence activators:** Synthetic chemicals that, when applied to plants as sprays, injections, root treatments, etc., induce systemic acquired resistance in them to several types of pathogens.

- **Deletion:** Absence of a segment of a chromosome, reducing the number of loci.

- **Deletion Mapping:** The use of overlapping deletions to locate a gene on a chromosome or a genetic map.

- **Demicyclic rust:** The rust in which uredial stage is absent. eg. *Gymnosporangiumjuniperi* _ *virginianae-* cedar apple rust.

- **Demographic stochasticity:** the variability in population density arising from random differences among individuals in reproduction and survival; plays a major role in small populations where differences between individuals have large effects.

- **Denaturation:** The loss of native configuration of a macromolecule resulting from heat treatment, extreme pH changes chemical treatment, etc. Denaturation usually accompanied by loss of biological activity. Denaturation of protein often results in an unfolding of the polypeptide chains and renders the molecule less soluble. Denaturation of DNA leads to changes in many of its physical propertiesdeuteromycete or a mitosporic fungus.

- **Deposition:** uniting of inoculum with a host after transport.

- **Deuteromycotina:** Thallus: septate mycelium. Motile spores are absent.

Sexual spores are absent. Asexual spores called conidia are present.

- **Dextrose:** a simple sugar found in fruit and also extracted from corn starch.

- **Dieback:** a fungal disease of some plants which kills shoots or branches anda gradual dying of trees starting at the ends of branches.

- **Digital organisms:** Self-replicating computer programs that compete with one another for central processing unit cycles, their only limiting resource for replication.

- **Dikaryon :**A pair of genetically different nuclei, lying side by side with out fusion for a considerable period of time is called dikaryon.A cell containing dikaryon is called **dikaryotic cell**.

- **Dilution end-point:**the lowest dilution in a serial dilution of a virus preparation that will infect a mechanically inoculated plant.

- **Dimer:** A compound having the same percentage composition as another but twice the molecular weight; one formed by polymerization

- **Dimorphism:** Two different forms in a group as determined by such characteristics as sex, size or coloration

- **Dioecious fungi:** The fungi which produce distinguishable male and female sex organs on two different thalliie., there will be separate male and female thalli.

- **Diploid:** An organism or cell with two sets of chromosomes (2n) or two genomes; somatic tissues of higher plants and animals are ordinary diploid in chromosomes constitution in contrast with the haploid (monoploid) gametes.

(or)

Diploid: referring to an organism that has two matched sets of chromosomes in a cell nucleus, one set from each parent (NOTE: Each species has a characteristic diploid number of chromosomes.)

- **Discontinuous resistance:** a response involving distinctive, clearcut symptoms in a segregating population, which is often controlled by a single dominant gene.

- **Disease control:** the systems put in place by a farm or a government to prevent diseases from spreading within the area under their supervision.

- **Disease dynamics:** the study of the change, growth or activity of a disease.

- **Disease gradient:** the change in incidence of a disease with increasing distance from the source of infection.

- **Disease resistance (Immunization):** Preventing infection or reducing effect of infection by managing the host through improvement of resistance in it by genetic manipulation or by chemical therapy.

   (or)

- **Disease resistance:** It is the ability of a plant to overcome completely or in some degree the effect of a pathogen or damaging factor.

- **Disease tetrahedron:** analogous to the disease triangle, in which the area symbolizes likelihood of disease, the disease tetrahedron is a visualization of the components' (abiotic) environment, host, pathogen, and additional biotic factors and their interactions responsible for plant disease development.

- **Disease Triangle:** The interactions of three components of disease, i.e., the host, pathogen and environment, can be visualized as a disease triangle. The length of each side is proportional to the sum total of the characteristics of each component that favour disease.

- **Disease:** a condition of a living organism that impairs normal functioning

   (or)

Disease: Any malfunctioning of host cells and tissues that result from continuous irritation by a pathogenic agent or environmental factor and leads to development of symptoms (G.N.Agrios, 1997)

- **Disease-suppressive soils:** soils in which a pathogen does not establish or persist, or in which it causes disease at first but then disease declines with successive cropping of the host.

- **Disinfectant:** A physical or chemical agent that frees a plant, organ, or tissue from infection.

  (or)

  Disinfestant: An agent that kills or inactivates pathogens in the environment or on the surface of a plant or plant organ before infection takes place.

- **Disorder:** Non-infectious plant diseases due to abiotic causes such as adverse soil and environmental conditions are termed disorders. The common characteristic of noninfectious diseases of plants is that they are caused by the lack or excess of something (temperature, soil moisture, soil nutrients, light, air and soil pollutants, air humidity, soil structure and pH) that supports life. Non-infectious plant diseases occur in the absence of pathogens, and cannot, therefore, be transmitted from diseased to healthy plants.

- **Dispersal:** movement of pathogen into another area.

- **Dispersing agent:** a chemical added to a fungicide/bactericide formulation to allow particles of the active agent to be distributed effectively.

- **Distortion:** malformed plant tissues

- **Diversifying selection:** natural selection that favors the fixation of advantageous mutations resulting in adaptive molecular evolution.

  (or)

  Diversifying selection: adaptive evolution based on positive selection of new amino acid sequence variants. Opposite of purifying selection that favors sequence conservation.

- **DNA barcoding:** an approach to specimen identification achieved using unique DNA sequences.

- **Dolipore septum:** Both primary and secondary mycelium consists of dolipore septum. The septum around the central pore swells at the center forming a barrel shaped structure with open ends,thus forming a septal pore. The septal pore is surrounded by a cup like or dome shaped membrane called parenthosome or septal pore cap or nuclear pore cap. It is made up of a double membrane and its function is to shut the pore

- **Domain:** A sequence of amino acid within a protein that can be identified with a particular function.

- **Dormancy:** an inactive period (or) Dormancy: Reduced physiological activity in a pathogen due to adverse environmental conditions.

- **Dough stage:** stage in ripening wheat caryopsis when endosperm develops a mealy or dough-like consistency.

- **Downy mildew:** a disease (*Perenospora brassica*) which causes white bloom on the under surface of leaves, most damaging to Brassica seedlings.

- **Dressing:** the process of treating seeds before sowing, to control disease.

- **Dry seed dressing:** This method is simple and economical. The method consists of adding the required fungicide (usually 0.3 %) to the seeds and shaking them in a closed vessel or a 'rotary drum' for 5-15'minutes to facilitate even spreading of fungicides over the surface of all seeds.

- **Dual culture:** To grow the antagonistic organism and pathogenic organism on the same plates, this is called as dual culture techniques. These techniques can be used for testing antibiotic production on as well as to study the mycoparasitism and lysis of

pathogen propagules and bio-agents.

- **Durable resistance:**used to describe resistance that is long lasting

- **Dusts (D):** Dust formulations usually contain 1-10% active ingredient for direct application in dry forms. They are manufactured in such a way that they are light enough to be carried by a slight breeze for a considerable distance. The finely divided particle of active ingredient is carried on a carrier particle.

- **Dutch elm disease:** a fungal disease that kills elm trees, caused by *Ceratocystisulmi*and spread by a bark beetle.

- **E**cotoxicity: the degree to which a chemical released into an environment by human activities affects the organisms that live or grow there.

- **Ectophytic fungus:** If the fungal thallus is present on the surface of the host plant, it is called ectophytic

- **Effector molecule:** A molecule the affects (positively or negatively) the function of a regulatory protein

(or)

Effector molecules: Small molecules that combine with repressor molecules and activate or inactivate them with respect to their ability to combine with an operator gene

- **Effector protein:** a protein that is secreted by the pathogen and which interacts with the host to promote disease development or to trigger defenses.

- **Effector:** microbial secreted molecule for host manipulation. Effectors are typically proteins with amino-terminal secretion signals that either reside in the plant apoplast or enter the host cell by poorly characterized mechanisms. One role of effectors is the suppression of host immune responses. In some cases, secondary metabolites have effector activity (e.g. bacterial syringolin and coronatine).

(or)

Effector: pathogen delivered molecules into host cells to suppress immune responses and promote pathogen proliferation.

(or)

Effector: pathogen-derived molecule that manipulates the host cell thereby facilitating infection.When an effector is recognized by a plant and triggers defense it is called an elicitor.

(or)

Effectors: pathogen molecules that manipulate host cell structure and function thereby facilitating infection and/or triggering defense responses. Effectors can be elicitors and/or toxins. Unlike these, the term effector is neutral and does not imply a negative or positive impact on the outcome of the disease interaction.

- **Electron microscope:** Here the images are formed on a fluorescent screen by electron beam focused by magnets instead of lens, with a magnification of 1, 00,000. These are used for observation of viruses and ultra structures of cells.

- **Electrophoresis:** A technique used to separate molecules based on different rates of movements, induced by an applied electric.

- **Elicitor:** pathogen-derived molecule that triggers defense responses resulting in enhanced resistance to the pathogen. When recognition is mediated by an R (resistance) protein, it is also referred to as an Avr (avirulence) protein and when recognized by a PRR (Pathogen Recognition Receptor), as a PAMP (Pathogen-Associated Molecular Pattern).

(or)

Elicitors: Molecules produced by a pathogen that induce a defense response by the host.

(or)

Elicitors: pathogen molecules that trigger defense responses resulting

in enhanced resistance to the invading pathogen.

- **Encapsidation:** The enclosure ofa virus's nucleic acid genome within a protein shell.

- **Endemic**: Constantly present in a moderate to severe form and is confined to a particular country or district

(or)

- **Endemic:** persistence of disease in a population without external inputs.

- **Endophytes:** beneficial microbes living inside the plant

(or)

Endophytes:microorganisms (archaea, bacteria, fungi, oomycetes, protista) inhabiting the interior of plants (endosphere) irrespective of the function in association with the plant.

- **Endophytic fungus:** If the fungus penetrates into the host cell / present inside the host, it is called endophytic

- **Endospores:** Spores are resting bodies produced by some species of bacteria within the cell. (Resting bodies)

- **Endotoxin:** a poison from bacteria which passes into the body when contaminated food is eaten.

- **Enteric pathogens:** microbes that occur pathogenically in the intestine of human or animals

- **Enterobacteria:** a family of bacteria, including *Salmonella* and *Escherichia.*

- **Enveloped virus:**plant viruses of the reovirus and rhabdovirus groups which have an outer lipid-protein membrane surrounding the protein shell of the virus.

- **Environment:** The complex of physical and biotic factors within which an organism exists

- **Environmental stochasticity:** the variability arising from randomness of environmental factors,such as weather, on reproduction and survival of the individuals in a population; can have an effect even at large population density.

- **Environmental variance:** The portion of the phenotypic variance caused by differences in the environments to which the individuals in a population have been exposed

- **Enzyme:** A protein or ordered aggregate of proteins that catalyzes a specific biochemical reaction and is not itself altered in the process

- **Enzyme:** a protein substance produced by living cells which promotes a biochemical reaction in living organisms.

- **Epidemic or Epiphytotic disease:** A disease usually occurs widely but periodically in a destructive form is referred as epidemic or Epiphytotic disease.

- **Epidemic:** an infectious disease that spreads quickly through a large part of the population.

- **Epidemiologically linked:** epidemiological data link the disease to the consumption of a (or multiple) food(s). The short shelf life of fresh produce makes it difficult to isolate the causative agent from this type of food, and epidemiological studies often are used to trace back the source of contamination.

- **Epidemiology:** Generally, plant diseases are essentially a study of the rate of multiplication of a pathogen and spread of the disease caused by it in a plant population. Epidemiology deals with outbreaks and spread of diseases in population epidermal cells of the host. Eg. *Puccinia, Colletotrichum, Erysiphe*

- **Epiphytes:** beneficial microbes living on the plant surface, e.g., in the rhizosphere.

- **Epiphytic:** state by which microbes colonize the surfaces of plants without causing disease.

- **Epitope:** Antigenic determinant, the portion of antigen which interacts with the T cell receptor of the immunoglobulin

- **EPPO:** European and Mediterranean Plant Protection Organization.

- **Eradication**: Reducing, inactivating, eliminating or destroying inoculum at the source, either from a region or from an individual plant in which it is already established

- **Ergot:** a fungus that grows on cereals, especially rye, producing a mycotoxin which causes hallucinations and sometimes death if eaten. Genus: *Claviceps*.

- **Erythromycin:** an antibiotic used to combat bacterial infections.

- **Ethidium bromide:** A fluorescent molecule that binds to DNA and changes its density, used to purify spercoiled DNA molecules and to localize DNA in gel electrophoresis

- **ETI (EffectorTriggered Immunity):** plant immune responses triggered by R proteins upon recognition of cognate effectors, reinforcement of PTI, classically known as gene-for-gene resistance.

- **Etiologic agent:** organism that causes a disease.

- **Eucarpic:** If the thallus is differentiated into a vegetative part which absorbs nutrients and a reproductive part which forms reproductive structures, such thallus is called eucarpicthallus

- **Eumycota**: True fungi. Thallus is typically filamentous with cell wall. Plasmodium absent.

- **Euploid:** A cell having any number of complete chromosomes sets or an individual composed of such cells

- **Exclusion of inoculum**: Preventing the inoculum from entering or establishing in the field or area where it does not exist

- **Experimental evolution:** Experimental testing of hypotheses and theories of evolution under controlled laboratory conditions.

- **Externally seed borne**: Dormant spores on seed coat

- **F**acultative parasite: Having the ability to be a parasite.

(or)

Facultative parasite: Organisms which are usually saprophytic but have ability to become as parasites

- **Facultative saprophytes**: Organisms which are usually parasites but have ability to become saprophytes .Eg. *Ustilagomaydis*

- **Fairy ring:** a circle of darker coloured grass in a pasture, which is caused by fungi.

- **Fastidious vascular bacteria (RLO's).** Fastidious vascular bacteria are similar to bacteria in most respects but are obligate parasites or cannot be grown on routine bacteriological media.

- **Field resistance:**Resistance shown by a host plant under natural field conditions, even though the same host may be susceptible to the virus under experimental conditions

- **Filters:** Heat sensitive materials like vitamin solutions are sterilized by filtration technique as they are destroyed by heating at temperature normally used for sterilization e.g. Seitz filter.

- **Fingerprint:** The characteristic spot pattern produced by electrophoresis of the polypeptide fragments obtained through denaturation of a particular protein with a proteolytic enzyme

- **Fission:** The parent cell elongates,nucleus undergo mitotic division and forms two nuclei, then the contents divide into equal halves by the formation of a transverse septum and separates into two daughter cells. Eg. *Saccharomycescerevisiae*

- **Flag leaf:** the last leaf formed on a developing wheat plant.

- **Flagella** : (sing.flagellum)Flagella are thin, hair like delicate structures attached to a basal granule called blepharoplast in cytoplasm and these are the organs of motility in lower fungi and aquatic fungi.

(or)

Flagella: Flagella are the organs of bacteria which is responsible for motility.

- **Flagellated protozoans:** Protozoa are microscopic,non-photosynthetic, eukaryotic,flagellate motile,single celled animals.

- **Flagellin:** A receptor system for general elicitors very similar and common to plants and animals.

- **Flagging:** The loss of rigidity and drooping of leaves and tender shoots preceding the wilting of a plant.

- **flg22:** 22-amino acid elicitor active epitope of bacterial flagellin.

- **Fluctuation test:** A test to prove that genetic changes and mutations occur spontaneously *i.e.* independent of the environment.

- **Foot rot:** a disease of the horny parts and the soft tissue of feet of sheep. It occurs particularly in wet marshy and badly-drained pastures, and is caused primarily by the organism *Fusiformisnecrophorus*and sometimes *Fusiformisnodosus.* It makes sheep lame.

- **Force of infection:** rate at which susceptible hosts become infected.

- **Forceps:** It is used for taking infected plant materials while doing isolation.

- **Foregut:** anterior part of the alimentary canal.

- **Forest type:** defined by the predominant forest species associated with a geographic area or region, e.g., oak-hickory; spruce-fir.

- **Forma specialis (f. sp.):** A group of races and biotypes of a pathogen species that can infect only plants within a certain host genus or species.

(or)

Forma specialis: Taxonomic classifier for parasites below the species level. The term is used for pathogens (most frequently fungi) that (i) are adapted to a specific host species and (ii) show no or minimal morphological differences to its closest relatives at the species level. Owing to their strict host specialization, mating between different formaespeciales is impossible on their respective hosts, but is occasionally seen on shared alternate hosts, leading to fertile progeny.

- **Fragmentation:** It is the most common method. Hypha of fungus breaks into small pieces, each broken piece is called a fragment, which function as a propagating unit and grows into a new mycelium.The spores produced by fragmentation are called **arthrospores**(arthron=joint) (spora=seed) or oidia.

- **FT-ARDRA:** a culture-independent microbial community fingerprinting method by which phylogenetic assignments can be inferred.

- **Fumigant:** a chemical compound that becomes a gas or smoke when heated and is used to kill insects and fungi.

   (or)

Fumigation: disinfection by means of gas or fumes which penetrate into cracks and holes, aprocess that is probably more efficient that spraying or scrubbing.

- **Fungi**: Fungi are eukaryotic, spore bearing, achlorophyllous organisms that generally reproduce sexually and asexually and whose filamentous, branched somatic structures are typically surrounded by cell walls consisting chitin or cellulose or both with many organic molecules.

- **Fungicide:** a substance used to kill fungi.

- **Fungigation:** Application of fungicides to foliage or roots through the irrigation system.

- **Fungistat**: Some chemicals which do not kill fungi, but simply inhibit the fungus growth temporarily.

- **Fungus:** a simple plant organism such as yeast mushrooms or mould with thread-like cells and without green chlorophyll.

- **Funiculus:** the narrow stalk that attaches the ovary to the base of the flower.
- **Furrow application:** Fungicides are applied either as dusts or mixed with water to the furrow at the time of planting for control of diseases that occur at the base of the plant. This method 'requires' much less quantity of fungicides per hectare than broadcast method.
- **Galls:** abnormal, localized swellings or tumors, on leaf, stem or root tissue
- **Gametangia:** Sex organs of fungi are called gametangia containing gametes or gamete nuclei.
- **Gametangial contact (gametangy / oogamy):** Male and female gametangia come in contact. At the place of contact, dissolution of wall occurs and a fertilization tube is formed. The contents of male gametangium migrate into female gametangium through a pore or fertilization tube developed at the point of contact. The gametangia do not loose their identity.
- **Gametangial copulation:** The isogametangia come in contact, their intervening wall dissolves leading to fusion of entire contents of two contacting gametangia to form a single unit.Gametangialoose their identity. The protoplasts fuse and the unit increases in size.
- **Gametes**: Sex cells are called as gametes
- **Gene interaction:** Interaction between different genes residing within the same genome in the production of a particular phenotype
- **Gene knockout:** The disruption of a target gene by transformation or mutation and characterization of the function of the gene by assessing the phenotype of the resulting mutant.
- **Gene mapping:** Assignment of a locus to a specific chromosome and or determining the sequence of genes and their relative distances

from one another on a specific chromosome.

- **Gene silencing:** The interruption or suppression of the activity of a targeted gene that prevents it from coordinating the production of specific proteins.

- **Gene-for-gene hypothesis:**the concept that corresponding genes for resistance and virulence exist in the host and pathogen respectively

- **Gene-for-gene interaction:** genomic host pathogen interaction predicted from the hypothesis proposed by HH Flor on the basis of his studies on rust-resistant flax breeding.

- **Gene-for-gene resistance:** resistance based on the genetic interaction between a dominant plant resistance (R) gene and a complementary dominant pathogen avirulence (*Avr*) gene.

- **Genetic bottleneck:** reduction of a population/species and loss of genetic diversity associated with severe mortality or reproductive isolation from the main population(s).

- **Genetic distance:** Death of an individual without reproducing.

- **Genetic engineering:** The use of *in vitro* techniques in the isolation manipulation, recombination and expression of DNA.

- **Genetic map:** The linear arrangement of mutable sites on a chromosome as deduced from genetic recombination experiment.

- **Genetic Marker:** A gene whose phenotypic expression is usually easily discerned, used to identify an individual or a cell that carries it, or as a probe to mark a nucleus, chromosome or locus.

- **Genome sequencing:** The orderly reading of all the millions of nucleotides constituting the total DNA of a living organism.

- **Genome:** the infectious component of the virus

- **Genophore:** The chromosome equivalent in viruses, prokaryotes

- **Geographic origin:** implies the site of speciation and generally an area where individuals express the greatest genetic diversity.
- **Germ theory:** The proposal that infectious and contagious diseases are caused by germs (microorganisms).
- **Germ tube:** The early growth of mycelium produced by a germinating fungus spore.
- **Glass rod:** It is used for mixing or stirring any culture medium or any samples.
- **Glass slide:** It is often used to spread liquids evenly into something. An example would be to coat glass surfaces with liquids to look at them under a microscope. It is used to see the microorganisms under microscope.
- **Graduated cylinder:** It is used to measure approximate volume of culture medium or any samples.
- **Granules (Pellets):** Pellets are the formulations of the fungicide with inert materials formed into particles about the size of coarse sugar. The granules normally contain 3-10% of the active ingredient. Due to their size, the granules do not drift but have limited application being confined to soil and seed treatments.
- **Guanine:** A purine base found in DNA and RNA
- **Guard protein:** molecules that associate with both pathogen effectors and host resistance proteins to control activation of resistance gene-mediated defense responses.
- **Gum:** complex of sugary substances formed by cells in reaction to wounding or infection gummosis: production of gum by or in a plant tissue.

Hairpin: Describes a double

helical region formed by base pairing between adjacent nucleotide of singles stranded DNA.

- **Haploid number:** The gametic chromosome number symbolized by n

- **Haustoria:** specialized infection structures of biotrophicoomycete and fungal pathogens that invaginate into the plant cells but remain enveloped by a modified host cell membrane.

- **Haustorium:** It is a outgrowth of somatic hyphae regarded as special absorbing organ produced on certain hyphae by parasitic fungi for obtaining nourishment by piercing into living cells of host

- **Heat treatment:** the use of high temperatures, typically 45°C, to disinfest storage areas or containers against virus.

- **Helper componentproteinase (HC-Pro):** a nonvirion and multifunctional protein of viruses inthe family *Potyviridae*that mediates binding between virion and sites within the insect mouthparts during non-persistent transmission.

- **Helper virus:** Provides functions absent from a defective virus enabling the latter to complete the infective cycle during a mixed infection

- **Hemibiotroph**: The parasites which attack living tissues in the same way as biotrophs but will continue to grow and reproduce after the tissue is dead called as *facultative saprophytes*.

- **Hemipteran:** insect belonging to the order Hemiptera that includes aphids, whiteflies, leafhoppers, planthoppers, and true bugs, but not thrips.

- **Hemipteroids:** insects that include hemipterans and their close relatives, i.e., thrips, lice and plant lice.

- **Hemocoel:** body cavity of insects that contains the hemolymph and all internal organs

- **Hemolymph:** insect equivalent of blood

- **Herbivore-induced resistance:** enhanced defensive capacity of the entire plant against insect feeding; acquired upon local induction by an insect herbivore.

- **Hereditary disease:** A pathological condition caused by a mutant gene

- **Heteroduplex:** A DNA generated during genetic recombination by base pairing between complementary single strands from differential parental duplex molecules

- **Heteroecious rust:** If spore stages are formed on two unrelated hosts ie., pycnia and aecia on one host and the uredia and telia on the other host, such rusts are called heteroecious rusts and phenomenon is called heteroecism

- **Heterogametangia:** If gametangia differ morphologically in size and structure, they are called as heterogametangia

- **Heterogametes**: If gametes differ morphologically, they are called heterogametes

- **Heterogamy**: If gametes are dissimilar, one motile, another is non motile.

- **Heterokaryon:** A cell or individual having nuclei from genetically different sources, the result of cell fusion not accompanied by nuclear fusion

- **Heterokaryosis:** The condition in which a mycelium contains two genetically different nuclei per cell.

- **Heterothallic fungi:** Fungi producing compatible male and female gametes on physiologically distinct mycelia.

- **Hevein:** a chitin-binding protein from rubber latex.

- **Hexaploid:** A cell or organism with six complete sets of chromosomes

- **Hfr cell:** An *E. coli* cell in which an F plasmid in integrated into the chromosome, enabling transfer of part or all the chromosome to an F cell.

- **Hfr:** Highly frequency recombination; conjugation donor

in which the F conjugative plasmid is integrated in the chromosome.

- **HG Type:** the designation, based on a bioassay, of the virulence profile of a *Heteroderaglycines*population. The HG Type is a numerical designation referring to the sources of resistance in *Glycine max* (i.e., soybean germplasm lines) on which the nematode is able to develop.

- **Holocarpic:** If the thallus is entirely converted into one or more reproductive structures, such thallus is called holocarpicthallus

- **Horizontal gene transfer (HGT):** also called lateral gene transfer. A process by which a genomic region is transferred to another organism, e.g., by a transposon. HGT may occur between different species or between different vegetative incompatible lines.

- **Horizontal gene transfer:** the hypothesis that genes for parasitism or virulence were transferred to nematodes from bacteria.

(or)

Horizontal gene transfer: the transfer of DNA between bacterial genomes by mechanisms such as conjugation, transformation, and phage transduction.

(or)

Horizontal resistance: Partial resistance, equally effective against all races of a pathogen.

- **Horizontal resistance**: When the resistance is uniformly spread against all the races of a pathogen, then it is called horizontal/generalized/non-specific/field/qualitative resistance. Horizontal resistance is usually governed by several genes and is more stable.

- **Horizontally acquired islands (HAIs):** large regions of DNA potentially acquired by HGT that re-identifiable by, for example, changes in GC content or the presence of phage or plasmid remnants.

- **Host factors:** To achieve replication, viruses must co-opt specific host proteins to facilitate intracellular targeting, recruit viral RNA, and provide other functions.
- **Host jump:** colonization of a new host species that is phylogenetically distantly related to the species of the contemporary host range.
- **Host metapopulation:** an assemblage of spatially separated, host subpopulations.
- **Host range expansion:** colonization of a new host species that is phylogenetically closely related to the species of the current host range.
- **Host range:** The various kinds of host plants that may be attacked by a parasite.
- **Host shift/host jump:** the process by which a pathogen infects a new previously unaffected host species. In a host shift, the alternate host is a close relative of the former host, whereas a host jump involves a new host that is taxonomically very distant from the former host, e.g., from another class or order.
- **Host specific:** These are the metabolic products of the pathogens which are selectively toxic only to the susceptible host of the pathogen
- **Host topology:** arrangements of susceptible hosts or fields in the landscape.
- **Host–pathogen arms race:** rapid co-evolution of the pathogenic and immune arsenal in matching host–parasite pairs. The term is often used in the context of the fast co-evolution of cognate effector–NB-LRR protein pairs, as exemplified by the special evolutionary forces (e.g. positive selection) operating on the genes encoding these proteins.
- **Host-tracking:** the co-evolution of a pathogen with its host. By host-tracking the pathogen is likely to be younger than the host, in contrast to co-speciation where host and pathogen have diverged simultaneously.

- **Hot air oven:** It is working under the principle of dry heat. Commonly used for sterilizing glass wares. It is provided with 3-4 racks for keeping all the glass wares. The electric coil is fitted all sides of the oven. The sterilization is done at a temperature of $160°C$ for 2 hours.

- **Hot plate stirrer:** It is useful to stir the chemicals in water without heat to make suspension. It is fined with the stirrer and heat control. Stirring is done by creating magnetic field, which causes the bar magnet kept in the container to spin resulting in the stirring of the medium.

- **Hot spot:** A site which the frequencies of spontaneous mutation or recombination are greatly increased with respect to other sites in the same cistron; a chromosomal site at which the frequencies of mutations are differentially increased in response to treatment with a specific mutagen

- **HST:** host-selective (or -specific) toxins that is toxic to cultivars with a specific susceptibility gene.

- **Humus:** the fibrous organic matter in soil, formed from decomposed plants and animal remains, which makes the soil dark and binds it together.

- **Hyalosporae**: cell wall of conidia hyaline

- **Hybridization:** The mating of individual belonging to genetically disparate populations or to different species; the mating of any two unlike genotypes

- **Hybridoma:** A hybrid animal cell produced by the fusion of a spleen cell and a cancer cell and able to produce monoclonal antibodies and to multiply

- **Hydrolysis:** The enzymatic breakdown of a compound through the addition of water.

- **Hyperparasitism:** Direct parasitism or lysis and death of the pathogen by another micro-organism when the pathogen is in parasitic phase are known as hyperparasitism.

- **Hyperplasia:** a malformation caused by an increase in cell numbers. An abnormal increase in the size of an organ is· referred to as *hypertrophy*.

- **Hypersensitive reaction (HR):** strong local plant defense reaction including biochemical andstructural defense, which culminates in cell death.

(or)

Hypersensitive response (HR): a programmed cell death in plants that occurs locally in response to attempted invasion by some pathogens. It is characterized by the rapid production of reactive oxygen intermediates and collapse of the plant cell, thereby preventing further infection specifically by biotrophic pathogens.

(or)

Hypersensitive response (HR): gene-for-gene resistance is often associated with a local cell death response at the site of infection.

This form of programmed cell death is referred to as the hypersensitive response.

- **Hypersensitivity:** Excessive sensitivity of plant tissues to certain pathogens. Affected cells are killed quickly, blocking the advance of obligate parasites

- **Hypertrophy:** A plant overgrowth due to abnormal cell enlargement.

- **Hypha:** Hypha is a thin, transparent, tubular filament filled with protoplasm.It is the unit of a filamentous thallus and grows by apical elongation

- **Hyphal anastomosis:** the union of a hypha with another resulting in cytoplasmic exchange.

- **Hypoplasia:** a malformation caused by a reduction in cell numbers. A reduction in organ size is called *atrophy*.

- **Hypovirulence:** attenuated fungal virulence mediated by virus infection, mitochondrial defects,or mutations in the fungal genome.

(or)

Hypovirulence: Reduced virulence of a pathogen strain as a result of the presence of transmissible double-stranded RNA.

- **Immune:** referring to a person, other animal or plant that is not affected by a specific microorganism.
- **Immunity:** the natural or acquired ability of a person or other animal to resist a microorganism and the disease it causes.
- **Imperfect fungus:** A fungus that is not known to produce sexual spores; also known as ain a single particle
- **In vitro:** A latin word literally means in glass / living in test tube applied to any process carried out in sterile culture under controlled condition in the laboratory
- **In vivo:** a latin word literally means in living applied to any process occur in a whole organism under field condition where there is no control over the environmental conditions
- **Inaccessibility:** cellular conditioning toward a rejection reaction induced by incompatible races or non-pathogens.
- **Inclusion bodies:** Crystalline or amorphous structures in virus-infected plant cells that are produced by and consist largely of viruses and are visible under a compound microscope.

(or)

Inclusion body: Virus induced structures that may occur in the cytoplasm or nucleus of infected plants.

- **Incomplete dominance:** occurs when a dominant gene is only partially expressed in the phenotype of the heterozygote.
- **Inconsequential virus-host interactions:** interactions that do not contribute to a successful infection but can affect host physiology.

- **Incubation period:** The period of time (or time lapse) between penetration of a host by a pathogen and the first appearance of symptoms on the host. It varies with pathogens, hosts and environmental conditions

(or)

- **Incubation period:** The period of time between penetration of a host by a pathogen and the first appearance of symptoms on the host.

- **Incubation:** period between infection and disease symptom expression in host.

- **Incubator:** It is used for incubation (culturing of microbes) at a constant temp. It is similar to an oven in construction and consists of an insulated cabinet fitted with a heating element at the bottom. The temp, of the incubation is maintained at desired level (ambient to $110°C$) by an automatic device called thermostat.

- **Individual:** used here for pathogen biomass resulting from one infectious unit when it is successful in infecting a host, for example, a lesion resulting from one spore.

- **Induced systemic resistance (ISR):** enhanced defensive capacity of the entire plant against a broad spectrum of pathogens; acquired upon local induction by beneficial microbes.

(or)

Induced systemic resistance: an activation of plant defense mechanisms by specific strains ofNon-pathogenic bacteria

(or)

Induced systemic resistance: the phenomenon that plants acquire an enhanced defensive capacity against subsequent pathogen attack as a result of root colonization by selected strains of non-pathogenic bacteria

- **Induction:** Refers to the ability of bacteria to synthesiscertain enzymes only when theirsubstrates are present, applied to gene expression, refers to switching on transcription as a result of interaction of the inducer with the regulator protein

- **Infection** is the establishment of parasitic relationship between two organisms, following entry or penetration (or) the establishment of a parasite within a host plant.

(or)

- **Infection:** the process of a microorganism entering a host organism and causing disease.

- **Infectious disease:** A disease that is caused by a pathogen that can spread from a diseased to a healthy plant.

- **Infectious dose:** the number of infecting organisms needed to cause disease.

- **Inhibitor:** Any substance or object that retards a chemical reaction, a major or modifier gene that interferes with a reaction

- **Injury profile:** a given combination of injury levels caused by a range of pests during a crop cycle.

- **Injury:** any observable deviation from the normal (healthy) crop; injury may lead to crop loss (damage).

- **Innate immunity:** summarizes mechanism of metazoan non-adaptive immunity. Shares principal and structural features with nonspecific and specific plant resistance.

- **Inoculation access period (IAP):** the period of time given for the vector to transmit the virus.

- **Inoculation loop:** It consist of a handle provided with screw device at one top of which holds a heat resistant platinum wire nichrome.

- **Inoculation needle:** Inoculation needle are used to transfer fungi or bacteria into Petri dishes. The inoculating needle must first be sterilized to rid itself of any unwanted bacteria or fungi, by heating over an open flame.

- **Inoculation:** an injection against a particular disease (or) the arrival or transfer of a pathogen onto a host.
- **Inoculum potential**: The energy of growth of a parasite available for infection of a host at the surface of the host organ to be infected (or) The resultant of the action of environment, the vigor of the pathogen to establish an infection, the susceptibility of the host and the amount of inoculums present
- **Inoculum**: It is the part of the pathogen which on contact with susceptible host plant causes infection (or) the infective propagules which on coming in contact with the host plant causes an infection are known as inoculums

(or)

Inoculum: The pathogen or its parts that can cause infection; that portion of individual pathogens that are brought into contact with the host.

- **Inorganic fungicide:** a fungicide made from inorganic substances such as sulphur.
- **Insect vector:** an insect that transmits a disease-inducing organism or agent.
- **Interaction disease model:** specific interactions between virus and host components disrupt host physiology to cause disease.
- **Internally seed borne**: Dormant mycelium under the seed coat or in the embryo
- **Inter-specific competition:** competition for resources between individuals of different species
- **Inter-specific:** involving two or more species.
- **Intra-specific:** occurring within a species.
- **Invasion:** The arrival of large numbers of unwanted organisms into an area.
- **Invasive species:** exotic, nonnative organisms that negatively affect the habitats they colonize.

(or)

- **Invasive species:** species nonnative to the ecosystem under consideration and its introduction causes economic or environmental harm or harm to human health.
- **IPPC:** International Plant Protection Convention.
- **Isogamy:** If both gametes are motile and similar.

- **J**asmonic acid/jasmonate (JA): plant hormone essential for the immune response against necrotrophic pathogens and herbivorous insects.
- **Juvenile:** any one of four immature stages of a plant-parasitic nematode.

- **K**aryogamy: The fusion of nuclei, usually of the two gametes in fertilization, syngamy

  (or)
- **Karyogamy**: union of 2 sexually compatible nuclei brought together by plasmogamy to form a diploid nucleus (2n) i.e., zygote
- **Keystone pathogens:** highly adapted pathogens directly manipulating plant defense with a strong influence on microbiome composition.
- **Koch's postulates:**criteria proposed by Koch for proving the pathogenicity of an organism: (1) the suspected causal organism must be constantly associated with the disease; (2) it must be isolated and grown in pure culture; (3) when inoculated into a healthy plant it must reproduce the original disease.

- **L**ambda Page: A double stranded DNA virus that infect *E. coli* once inside the host cell, the lambda genome can enter a lysogenic cycle or a lytic cycle, which pathway is chosen depends upon an intricate balance of host and viral factors.

- **Laminar air flow chamber:** The cabinet is made up of stainless steel. The walls of the glass are made up of plexi glass. The unit is fitted with pre filter and HEPA filter (high efficiency particulate air). Size of HEPA filter is 0.3μ

- **Land-races:**stocks of plants selected by farmers on a local basis over many years, which are strongly adapted for local conditions.

- **Latency:** period between infection of host and production of inoculum.

- **Latent infection:** Latent infection refers to the conditions in which the plant pathogens may survive for a long time in plant tissue without development of visual symptoms

- **Latent period:**the period after a vector has acquired a virus before it can transmit it. Often observed in the case of persistent virus transmission.

(or)

- **Latent period:** The period during infection when the causative agent

cannot be detected by conventional techniques

- **Latent virus:** A virus that does not induce symptom development in its host.

- **LD 40:** The radiation dose required to kill half of a population of organisms within a specified time

- **Leaf blotch:**a disease of cereals *(Rhynchosporiumsecalis)* where dark grey lesions with dark brown margins occur on the leaves

- **Leaf spot:** A fungal disease of brassicas, where the leaves develop brown and black patches

- **Lesion:** An open wound on the surface of a plant or on the skin of an animal, caused by disease or physical damage

- **Lesion-mimic mutants:** plants that " spontaneously " develop necrotic lesions during development or in response to variations in environmental conditions

- **Leucine:** an essential amino acid

- **Light microscope:** Specimen is illuminated by visible light or U.V.

rays with a max magnification of 1000 or more. These are used for observing stained and unstained specimens and counting of microbes. They include the bright field, dark field, U.V phase contrast and the fluorescent microscope.

- **Lignin:** The material in plant cell walls that makes plants woody and gives them rigidity and strength

- **Liquid medium:** It does not contain a gelling or solidifying agent

- **Liquid nitrogen:** Cultures, tissue spore suspension are treated with a protective medium such as 10% sterilized glycerol or 10% dimethyl sulfoxide placed in glass bottles under store at ultra low temperature (-1960C) in liquid nitrogen.

- **Lithotroph:** Organisms which use inorganic electron donor

- **Locus:** The position of a gene on a chromosome

- **Longevity end-point:** the storage time after which a virus in a crude sap preparation loses its infectivity. Usually determined at 0 or 20°C.

- **Loose smut:** A fungus *(Ustilagonuda)* affecting wheat and barley. Masses of black spores collect on the diseased heads; the spores are dispersed in the wind, and only a bare stalk is left

- **Loss:** any decrease in economic returns from damage, and the cost of agricultural activitiesdesigned to reduce damage.

- **LPS:** lipo-polysaccharides, an active component involved in initial recognition.

- **Lysogeny:** A phenomenon in which the genome of a temperate phage establishes a stable non-lytic presence in its living host without producing progeny virions

- **Lysozyme:** an enzyme that cleaves bacterial peptidoglycans

- **Lytic cycle:** Multiplication of a bacteriophage within a host cell leading to lysis of cell and re-infection of other sensitive bacteria

- **Macrocyclic rust:** Rusts in which all 5 spore forms are produced or produce at least one type of binucleate spore in addition to teleospores are called macrocyclic rusts. It may be autoeciousmacrocyclic rust or heteroecious , macrocyclic rust

- **Malignant:** tissue that divides and enlarges autonomously, forming a tumor or gall

- **MAMP:** abbreviation for 'Microbe-Associated Molecular Pattern'. A MAMP is ahighly conserved molecule (e.g. protein or carbohydrate) that is specific for a taxonomic group of parasites and that triggers an immune response in a host by its recognition via Pattern Recognition Receptors.

- **Management**: It conveys a concept of continuous process which is based not only on the principle of eradication of the pathogen but mainly on the principle of minimizing the damage or loss below economic injury level

- **Mapping:** The process of collecting information and using it to produce maps.

- **Masked symptoms:** virus-induced plant symptoms that are normally, but appear when the host is exposed to certain environmental conditions of light and temperature

- **Mastigomycotina:** Thallus is unicellular or aseptate mycelium.Asexual spores are zoospores (motile spores).Sexual spores are oospores. Sexual reproduction by gametangial contact.

- **Maturation:** development of reproductive structures by a pathogen.

- **Mechanical transmission:**used to describe artificial transmission of a virus in which an infectious preparation is rubbed onto a test plant. May also occur in the field when virus is transmitted from one plant to another by leaves rubbing or root contact.

- **Meiosis**: This is reduction division. The number of chromosomes is reduced to haploid (n) i.e., diploid nucleus results into haploid nucleus

- **Melanin:** A dark brown to black compound found in the cell walls of some fungi and needed by them for pathogenicity.

- **Meristem culture:** culture of a shoot apical meristem in view of avoiding contaminations, especially specific viruses and bacteria

- **Methanol:** An alcohol manufactured from coal, natural gas or waste wood, which is used as a fuel or solvent. Formula: CH_3OH. Also called methyl alcohol, wood alcohol.

- **Methyl bromide:** An effective chemical for sterilizing soil and fumigating spaces

- **Micro pipette**: They are one standard laboratory equipment used to measure and transfer small volumes of liquids.

- **Microbial ecology:** The study of the way in which microbes develop in nature

- **Microbiome:** communities of commensal, mutualistic, and pathogenic microorganisms that live in close association with a host. **(or)**

- **Microbiome:** genomes of all microorganisms sharing a given environment.

- **Microbiota:** all microorganisms sharing a given environment.

- **Microcyclic rust (short cycled rust):**Rusts which produce no binucleate spore other than teleosporei.e., teleospore is the binucleate spore produced and both aecia and uredia are lacking

- **Micrometer:** One millionth of a meter (10^{-6}m), the unit used for measuring microorganisms; a device used for the measurement of (a part) of specimen

- **Microscope:** Microscope is a device, which can magnify a microbial cell or a group of

microbial cells to enable the human eye to study its structures, morphology etc.

- **Mildew:** a plant disease in which the pathogen is seen as a growth on the surface of the host; e.g., downy mildew, powdery mildew, caused by very different fungi, but both having the name Mildew.

- **Mitosporic fungi:** Producing spores only through mitosis

- **Mobilisation:** Conjugative transfer of non-conjugation plasmid in the presence of conjugative plasmid

- **Mode of action:** The way in which a pesticide acts. For example, organo phosphorous compounds disrupt the nerve impulses in insects

- **Molecular marker:** A molecular characteristic (a landmark) on a piece of DNA that can be used to compare that DNA for degrees of similarity with those of other microorganisms.

- **Mono-, bi-, and tripartite viruses:** one, two, or three genomecomponents, respectively, required to initiate infection.

- **Monoclonal antibodies:** Identical antibodies produced by a single clone of lymphocytes and reacting only with one of the antigenic determinants of a pathogen or protein.

- **Monocyclic disease:** disease that completes only one life cycle (sporulation, dispersal, infection, colonization, symptoms) during a cropping season; new spores often develop on crop debris during the intercrop period.

- **Monoecious fungi / hermaphroditic fungi:** The fungi which produce distinguishable male and female sex organs on the same thallus, which may or may not be compatible are called monoecious/ hermaphroditic fungi

- **Monogenic resistance**: When the defense mechanism is controlled by a single gene pair, it is called monogenic resistance.

- **Monophagous:**when an insect such as an aphid feeds on a specific type of host plant
- **Mortar and pestle:** It is used to grind any plant samples into a paste or powder form.
- **Mosaic:** symptom of certain viral diseases of plants characterized by intermingling patches of normal green and light green or yellowish colors
- **Mottle:** an irregular pattern of indistinct light and dark green areas
- **Multi-component virus:**a virus whose genome is divided into two or more parts, each part being separately encapsidated. Hence two or more components are needed to initiate an infection. Note that this is different to a multipartite genome where components may be enclosed
- **Multiplex PCR:** a PCR method based on mixtures of more than one primer pair to amplify more than one target.
- **Multisite fungicide:** A fungicide that is active against different metabolic pathways. e.g. Copper and Sulphur fungicides
- **Mutualism:** mutual beneficial relationship between host and microorganism.
- **Mycelium:** A mass of hyphae which forms the main part of a fungus

(or)

- **Mycelium:** A net work of hyphae (aggregation of hyphae) constituting the filamentous thallus of a fungus.It may be colourless i.e., hyaline or coloured due to presence of pigments in cell wall.The mycelium may be ectophytic or endophytic
- **Mycology:** The study of fungi
- **Mycorrhiza:** A mutual association of a fungus with the roots of a plant in which the fungus supplies the plant with water and minerals and feeds on the plant's sugars
- **Mycosis:** An infection with or a disease caused by fungi

- **Mycotoxin:** A toxic substance produced by a fungus growing on crops in the field or in storage.

(or)

Mycotoxins: Toxic substances produced by several fungi in infected seeds, feeds, or foods; and capable of causing illnesses of varying severity and death to animals and humans that consume such substances

- **Mycovirus:** a virus that infects fungi (or) viruses that infects and replicate in fungi.

- **Myxomycota:** Plasmodial forms without cell wall. Plasmodium is a naked multinucleate mass of protoplasm which moves and feeds in an amoeboid direction. Also calledas slime molds

- **N**atural **medium:** The exact chemical composition of this media isn't known properly. It includes ingredients of natural origin like yeast extract, beef, milk, tomato juice, blood etc.

- **NB-ARC:** nucleotide binding (NB) domain shared between human APAF-1 (Apoptotic Protease-Activating Factor 1), some plant R proteins, and CED-4 (*Caenorhabdituselegans*Dead protein 4).

- **NB-LRR proteins:** intracellular host proteins that recognize strain/isolate/race specific effectors, thereby initiating an immune response, which frequently results in localized host cell death (hypersensitive response). NB-LRR proteins occur in an accession-specific manner and, together with the recognized effectors, are main drivers of the host-pathogen arms race.

- **Neck rot:** A disease affecting bulb onions during storage. The onions become soft and begin to rot from the stem downwards

- **Necrosis:** The death of tissue or cells in an organism

- **Necrotroph**: A parasite is a *necrotroph*when it kills the host

tissues in advance of penetration and then lives saprophytically. Ex: *Sclerotiumrolfsii.*

- **Nematode feeding site:** after invading the root, root-knot and cyst nematodes induce formation of a permanent feeding site within cells close to the phloem.

- **Network:** a large and distributed group of individuals or organizations that exchange information and work toward a common goal.

- **Niche:** the functional position of an organism within its community regarding its interactions with the biotic and abiotic environment

- **Nicotine:** A harmful substance in tobacco. It is used as an insecticide

- **Non persistent virus:** A virus which is not retained for not more than a few hours by vectors

- **Non-cellautonomous proteins (NCAPs):** molecules that move via the plasmodesmata to affect physiological functions in adjacent or distant cells.

- **Non-circulative transmission:** viruses are acquired externally by their vectors without circulating through the bodies of the vectors

- **Non-host resistance:** resistance of all ecotypes of a given plant species to all races of a pathogenspecies

(or)

Non-host resistance: resistance to pathogens that are virulent on other host plants, no macroscopic symptoms, PTI/weak ETI contribute to nonhost resistance.

- **Non-persistent pesticide:** A pesticide which does not remain toxic for long, and so does not enter the food chain

(or)

Non-persistent transmission: a mode of transmission that is accomplished by acquisition access of seconds to a few minutes and generally retention by the vector for no more than a few minutes to hours.

- **Non-persistent viruses:** plant viruses for which inoculativity by

the vector is retained for only a few seconds/minutes after acquisition from plants and is also lost after molting.

- **Non-self recognition:** the ability of an organism to recognize molecules that originates from other species or individuals.

- **Non-specific:** These are the metabolic products of the pathogen, but do not have host specificity and affect the protoplasm of many unrelated plant species that are normally not infected by

- **Northern blot analysis:** Determines whether the transcript or the messenger RNA (mRNA) of the introduced DNA is present and is correctly transcribed in the transgenic plant. The messenger RNA of the transgenic plants are isolated and processed to bind to the nitrocellulose membrane. Labeled DNA is used to bind to the mRNA and can be visualized through autoradiography.

- **NPPO:** national plant protection organization.

- **NPR1:** redox-sensitive transcriptional regulator of SA-dependent responses, mediator of SA-JA cross talk, and regulator of SAR and ISR.

- **O**bligate biotroph: an organism that only obtains nutrients from living host cells and commonly cannot be cultured.

- **Obligate parasite:** a pathogen capable of living only as a parasite and which cannot be cultured on an artificial medium.

(or)

Obligate parasites: Organisms which obtain food only from living organisms (living protoplasm) and can never derive their food from dead organic matter or artificial medium. Eg. *Pucciniagraminis, Plasmoparaviticola.*

- **Obligate saprophytes:** Organisms which can never grow on living organisms or can never obtain their

food from living source. They get their food only from dead organic matter

- **Ocular Micrometer:** It is a simple glass disc with etched lines on its surfaces. It has 100 equally space divisions measuring 0 to 100. The distance between graduations of an ocular micrometer does not have only standard value in depending on the objects used.

- **OECD:** Organization for Economic Cooperation and Development

- **Oidiopsis**: Mycelium is endophytic. Conidiophores may be branched or unbranched, erect, septate, hyaline and emerge through stomata. Conidia are produced singly and cylindrical in shape. Conidia are of two types. a. blunt tip b. pointed tip.

- **Oidium:** Mycelium is ectophytic, hyaline. Conidia are developed from a flask shaped mother cell (spore mother cell) formed on a short conidiophore. Conidia are barrel shaped with flat ends and are

produced in chains. The conidia are also referred to as meris tem arthrospores as these are formed by fragmentation of hyphae

- **Oligogenic resistance**: when the defense mechanism is governed by a few gene pairs, it is called oligogenic resistance.

- **Oogonium / Ascogonium:** The female gametangium is called Oogonium (oomycetes) or ascogonium (ascomycotina). Female gametangium is large and globose shaped

- **Oospore:** A thick walled sexual resting spore produced by the union of two morphologically different gametangia

(or)

- **Oospore:** A thick walled sexual resting spore produced by the union of two morphologically different gametangia. Eg.*Pythium, Phytophthora*

- **Ooze:** a mass of bacterial cells usually embedded in a slimy matrix appearing on the diseased plant surface, often as a droplet; or, a flux, a viscid mass of juices composed of host and parasite substances occasionally found exuding from a diseased plant

- **Operon:** A cluster of functionally related genes regulated and transcribed as a unit.

- **Opportunistic pathogen:** an organism causing disease only when resistance in the host is lowered.

- **Orthologs:** related genes in different species.

- **Osmotin:** a basic PR-5 protein that is induced by osmotic stress

- **Outbreak:** the sudden increase in the incidence of a disease above what would be expected ata given time and geographic scale

- **Ovulariopsis:**Mycelium is partly ectophytic and partly endophytic. The conidiophores are hyaline, septate, unbranched, and bear a single conidium. Conidia are rhomboid in shape.In some species,the conidiiphores are spiral in shape.

- **P**ackaging or encapsidation: assembly of nucleic acid sequence into a virion.

- **Packaging signal:** an RNA sequence required to specifically interact with CP to mediate packaging of that sequence into a virion.

- **PAMP/MAMP (pathogen-/microbeassociated molecular pattern):** microbederived, highly conserved structures, recognized by PRRs to elicit immune responses, allow discrimination between self and non-self.

- **Pandemic:** an epidemic that spreads worldwide or across large geographical regions.

- **Parafilm:** It is used to cover or seal the Petri plates or test tubes.

- **Parallel testing:** testing or screening for a number of pathogens at one time, usually with

multiple tests performed side by side.

- **Paralogs:** homologous genes within a species

- **Paraphyses**: These are elongated, cylindrical; club shaped or sometimes branched threads arising from bottom of ascocarp. They may be septate or aseptate. They grow among asci in hymenium and remain free at their tips

- **Paraphysoids**: These are inter ascal tissue that stretch and resemble pseudoparaphyses, but remotely septate,very narrow,anastomose and tips remain free

- **Parasexual hybridization**: Hybridization by non-sexual methods. Eg:- protoplast fusion

- **Parasexuality**:Parasexual cycle is a process in which plasmogamy, karyogamy and haploidisation (non meiotic process) takes place in a sequence but not at specified points in the life cycle of a fungus. It was first discovered in 1952 by Pontecorvo and Roper in *Aspergillusnidulans.*

- **Parasite:** Organisms which derive the materials they need for growth from living plants are called parasites

(or)

Parasites: Organisms which live within or outside another organisms for their nutrition either completely or for a part of their life

- **Parasitism:** symbiotic relationship that is beneficial to one organism and harmful to the other organism.

- **Paring and Pralinage:** It is used to control *Fusarium*wilt and burrowing nematode (*Radopholussimilis)* of banana. The roots as well as a small portion of corm is removed or chopped off with a sharp knife and the sucker is dipped in 0.1% carbendazim solution for 5 minutes. Then, the sucker is dipped in clay slurry and furadan granules are sprinkled over the corm @ 40 g/corm.

- **Pathobiome:** a pathogen, its surrounding microbial community, and their interactions leading to plant disease.
- **Pathobionts:** members of the microbiome normally living in commensal or mutualistic relationship but acting as pathogens after breakdown of the plant-microorganism balance; includes necrophytic and saprophytic microorganisms.
- **Pathogen detection:** the identification of microorganisms or their products, e.g., toxins, in any number of substrates including plant tissues, soil, and water.
- **Pathogen surveillance:** the monitoring of plant systems for pathogens and/or diseases.
- **Pathogen:** An entity, usually a micro-organism that can incite disease. In a literal sense a pathogen is any agent that causes *pathos* (ailment, suffering) or damage. However, the term is generally used to denote living organisms (Fungi, bacteria, MLO's, nematodes etc.,) and viruses but not nutritional deficiencies

(or)

Pathogen: is an entity usually a micro organism that can incite disease in susceptible plants. It is also referred to as incident, causal agent or causal organism

- **Pathogenesis** is the chain of events that lead to development of disease in the host (or) sequence of progress in disease development from the initial contact between the pathogen and its host to the completion of the syndrome

(or)

Pathogenesis: interactions between pathogen and host resulting in disease.

- **Pathogenicity** is the ability of the pathogen to cause disease
- **Pathogenicity Island:** a distinct class of genomic islands that are acquired by horizontal transferand encode genes that contributes to virulence.

- **Pathotoxins**: These are the toxins which play a major role in disease production and produce all or most of the symptoms characteristic of the disease in susceptible plants. Most of these toxins are produced by pathogens during pathogenesis

- **Pathovar:** In bacteria, a subspecies or group of strains that can infect only plants within a certain genus or species.

  (or)

  Pathovar: taxonomic classifier for bacteria below the species level. Describes a set of bacterial strains that is differentiated from other strains of the same bacterial 'species' on the basis of their capacity to colonize distinct hosts.

- **Pattern recognition receptors:** host proteins that recognize conserved microbial molecules (MAMPs). They are typically membrane-bound receptor-like kinases with extracellular domains for MAMP detection/binding (e.g. leucine-rich repeats or carbohydrate-binding LysM domains).

- *pen* **mutant:** mutants susceptible to penetration by inappropriate powdery mildew pathogens

- **Penetration resistance:** the ability of a given plant to prevent invasion by fungal infection structures.

- **Penetration:** Pathogens penetrate plant surfaces by direct penetration or indirectly through wounds or natural openings. Bacteria enter plants mostly through wounds and less frequently through natural openings. Viruses, viroids, mollicutes, fastidious bacteria enter through wounds made by vectors. Fungi, nematodes and parasitic higher plants enter through direct penetration and less frequently through natural openings and wounds

- **Peptide library:** an ordered collection of peptides or peptide mixtures that contains and represents the sequence diversity of peptides of a given size or property.

The intrinsic order and organization of a peptide library permit individual bioactive sequences to be identified under appropriate assay conditions.

- **Perfect stage:** The sexual stage in the life cycle of a fungus; The teleomorph

- **Periphyses**: These are short, hair like threads lining in side of an ostiole of perithecium or pseudothecium. Their function is to direct the asci towards ostiole at the time of ascospore release

- **Periphysoids:** These are the lateral periphyses which are short and originate above the level of developing asci but do not reach base of cavity and curve upwards towards apex

- **Perithecium:** It is more or less closed ascocarp; but at maturity it is provided with ostiole through which the ascospores escape.

(or)

Perithecium; It is a flask shaped more or less closed ascocarp but provided with a pore or opening at the tip called true ostiole through which ascospores are released at maturity.Ostiole is lined inside with sterile structures called as periphysis. The wall is called peridium. The asci are arranged in definite layer called hymenium. In between the asci,there are sterile thread like structures called paraphyses which help in liberation of ascospores

- **Permatins:** proteins that permeabilize microbial membranes

- **Persistent virus:** A virus which retains for longer period (sometimes throughout life) by vector and sometimes pass to the progeny of vector and transmitted by mouth parts

(or)

Persistent viruses: plant viruses for which inoculativity by the vector is retained for long periods (days to weeks), often throughout the vectors lifespan, and also is retained after molting.

- **Petri plate:** A Petri dish (or Petri plate or cell culture dish) is a shallow glass or plastic cylindrical lidded dish that biologists use to culture living microorganisms. It was named after German bacteriologist Julis Richard Petri.

- **PGPF:** plant growth – promoting fungi.

- **PGPR:** plant growth – promoting rhizobacteria.

- **Phaeosporae**: cell wall of conidia coloured/ pigmented.

- **Phase transition:** an abrupt change from non-invading to invading state of an epidemic in response to small change in a critical parameter.

- **Phosphomannans:** phosphorylated mannose polymers.

- **Phyllosphere:** leaf surfaces or total above-ground surfaces of a plant. In this review, phyllosphere also includes the leaf interior

- **Phytoalexin:** A substance that inhibits the development of a fungus on hypersensitive tissue formed when host plant cells come in contact with the parasite.

(or)

Phytoalexins: Muller and Borger (1940) first used the term phytoalexins for fungistatic compounds produced by plants in response to injury (mechanical or chemical) or infection.

- **Phytoanticipins:** Inhibitory antimicrobial compounds present in plant cells before infection.

- **Phytoplasma**: Phytoplasmas are pleomorphic, wall less prokaryotic micro organisms, that can infect plants and cannot yet to be grown in culture

- **Phytosanitary:** referring to plant health, particularly freedom from diseases and pests.

- **Phytotoxins**: These are the substances produced in the host plant due to host-pathogen interactions for which a causal role in disease is merely suspected rather than established. These are the products of parasites which induce few or none of the symptoms caused by the living pathogen. They are non-specific and there is no relationship between toxin production and pathogenicity of disease causing agent.

- **Pipette:** It is used for measuring accurate quantity of plant sample liquids.

- **Planogametic copulation:** This involves the union of 2 naked gametes one or both of which are motile.

- **Plant disease diagnosis:** determination of the cause of a disease or syndrome in a plant or plant population.

- **Plant Disease:** It is the malfunctioning of host cells and tissue that results from continuous irritation by a pathogenic agent and leads to development of symptoms

- **Plant quarantine:** a legal restriction on the movement of agricultural commodities for the purpose of exclusion, prevention or delaying

the spread of the plant pests and diseases in uninfected areas.

- **Plantibodies:** Antibodies produced in transgenic plants expressing the antibody-producing gene(s) of a mouse that had been injected previously with a pathogen (usually a virus) that infects the plant.

(or)

Plantibodies: Transgenic plants have been produced which are genetically engineered to incorporate into their genome, and to express foreign genes, such as mouse genes that produce antibodies against certain plant pathogens

- **Plasmids:** Plasmids are small extrachromosomal, circular DNA elements which are capable of autonomous multiplication

- **Plasmogamy**: union of two protoplasts takes place. As a result of it the two nuclei come together within the same cell

- **Plectenchyma:** Fungal tissues are called plectenchyma i.e., mycelium becomes organized into loosely or compactly woven tissue. This tissue compose various types of vegetative and reproductive structures

- **Poisoned Food Technique:** The principle involved in this technique is to 'poison' the nutrient medium with afungi toxicant and then allow a test fungus to grow on such a medium. In this technique a solid or liquid medium can be used.

- **Polyclonal antibodies:** The usual mix of antibodies present in the serum of the blood of an animal that has been injected with a pathogen or protein that generally has many antigenic determinants.

- **Polycyclic disease:** disease that completes several life cycles during a cropping season.

- **Polycyclic:** Completes many (life or disease) cycles in one year.

- **Polyetic:** Requires many years to complete one life or disease cycle.

- **Polygenic resistance**: When the defense mechanism is controlled by many genesor more groups of supplementary genes, it is called polygenic resistance.

- **Polymerase chain reaction:** PCR is a quick test to determine if the regenerated transgenic cells or plants contain the gene. It uses a set of primers (DNA fragments) – forward and backward primers, whose nucleotide sequences are based on the sequence of the inserted gene. The primers and single nucleotides are incubated with the single stranded genomic DNA and several cycles of DNA amplification is conducted in a PCR machine.

- **Polyphagous:**when an insect such as an aphid feeds on various secondary host species

- **Polysaccharides:** Fungi, bacteria and nematodes release varying amounts of mucilaginous substances that coat their bodies and provide interface between the outer surface of the micro-organism and its environment. The role of slimy polysaccharides is of utmost importance in wilt diseases.

- **Poorly crystalline:** nanocrystalline or amorphous mineral phases that, because of their large surface area are highly bioavailable or reactive to aqueous solutions.

- **Postinvasive immunity:** inducible cellular defense responses provided by PTI/ETI that restrict pathogen in completion of their life cycle.

- **Predisposition:** It is the action of set of environments, prior to penetration and infection, which makes the plant vulnerable to attack by the pathogen. It is related to the effect of environments on the host, not on the pathogen, just before actual penetration occurs

- **Preinvasive immunity:** physical/chemical barriers and inducible reactions (PTI) preventing pathogens from gaining access to host tissue.

- **Pressure cooker:** It is a suitable alternative to an autoclave. Some labs will have a big size pressure cookers implanted with a pressure gauge. In case of power failure materials are sterilized in pressure cooker.

- **Primary infection:** The first infection of a plant by the overwintering or oversummering pathogen.

- **Primary inoculum:** The overwintering or over summering pathogen, or its spores that cause primary infection.

- **Priming:** sensitization of the whole plant for enhanced defense; characterized by a faster and stronger activation of cellular defenses upon invasion.

- **Probe DNA:** Probe DNA is the Specific cloned DNA sequence, which can be hybridize to complementary (related) ssDNAproducts such as vegetables, milk, and meat, by contaminating them on the farm or in the market with human pathogens. Also, scaring people for future shortages of food by spreading plant pathogens on crops so that terrorists reduce the amount of food produced.

- **Production situation:** the physical, biological, technical, social, and economic context in which agricultural production takes place. In order to address crop losses, as here, it is often convenient to exclude pests from the biological components of production situations.

- **Programmed cell death:** Death of specific cells of an organism, the initiation and execution of which is controlled by the organism.

- **Propagative virus:** a virus that multiplies within its insect vector.

  (or)

  Propagative viruses: viruses that invade and replicate in various tissues of their vectors

- **Prosenchyma:** It is a loosely woven tissue. The component hyphae retain their individuality which can be easily distinguishable as hyphae and lie parallel to one another

- **Proteasome:** A protein complex that is a part of a major catabolic pathway that degrades intracellular proteins after they have outlived their usefulness. The degradation process occurs in both the nucleus and the cytoplasm, and involves marking the target proteins through the addition of ubiquitin molecules (ubiquitination) for complete hydrolysis.

- **Protectant:** As the name suggests, protectant fungicides are prophylactic in their behavior. Fungicide which is effective only if applied prior to fungal infection is called a protectant, eg.,Zineb, Sulphur.

- **Protection**: The prevention of the pathogen from entering the host or checking the further development in already infected plants by the application of chemicals is called protection

- **Protein subunit:** A small protein molecule that is the structural and chemical unit of the protein coat of a virus.

- **Prototroph:** A nutritionally wild type of organism which does not require any additional growth supplement

- **Prototunicateascus:** This is the primitive type. The wall is very thin, dissolves at maturity and spores are released. The ascospores are released in a mucilaginous substance

- **PRR (pattern recognition receptor):** host encoded receptors recognizing microbial patterns (PAMPs) with high specificity and affinity to trigger immune responses (PTI).

- **Pseudoparaphyses:**These are distinct,vertical, paraphyses -like hyphae, that originate above the level of asci and grow downwards between the developing asci finally becoming attached to the base of the cavity, thus forming curtains

between asci. These are often broader, regularly septate, branched and anastomosing.

- **Pseudoparenchyma:**It is compactly woven tissue. It consists of closely packed cells which are isodiametric or oval in shape resembling parenchymatous cells of plants and hence the name. The component hyphae loose their individuality and are not distinguishable as hyphae

- **Pseudothecium:** stromatic fruiting body containing asci and ascospores, formed by members of a group of ascomycete fungal pathogens (loculoascomycetes)

- **PTI (PAMPtriggered immunity):** plant immune responses triggered by PAMPs, immediate, transient defense reactions.

- **Purification:** The isolation and concentration of virus particles in a pure form, free from cell components.

- **Pycnidium:** It is a globose or flask shaped fruiting body lined inside with conidiophores which produce conidia. It may be completely closed or may have an opening called ostiole.

(or)

Pycnidium: It is a hollow, flask shaped or globose fruiting body with a narrow mouth (*Ostiole*) whose pseudo parenchymatous inner walls (*Peridium*) are lined with conidiophore which bear conidia (eg) *Macrophomiaphaseolina, Botrydiplodiatheobromae, Diplodianatalensis.*

- **Q**uarantine: Control of import and export of plants to prevent spread of diseases and pests.

- **Quercus:** Species are taxonomically divided into three groups: red oak (section *Lobatae*), the white oak (section *Quercus*), and intermediate (section *Protobalanus*).

- **Quorum sensing (QS):** population density – dependent regulatory mechanism based on diffusible compounds regulating gene expression according to cell density.

(or)

Quorum sensing: a process that allows cell-to-cell communication in a wide variety of bacteria based on cell density-dependent regulation of various traits.

- **R** gene: specific major gene determining resistance response to pathogen races with a corresponding avirulence (*Avr*) gene.

- **Race:** designation of the virulence profile.

- **Receptor-Like Kinase (RLK):** an eLRR plasma membrane-spanning protein with a cytoplasmic protein kinase domain.

- **Receptor-Like Protein (RLP):** an eLRR protein with a short cytoplasmic domain lacking homology to a protein kinase domain.

- **Reciprocal best hit:** a consistent "top match" between two coding sequences following reciprocal FASTA analyses between two genomes.

- **Refrigerator:** It is a basic requirement in a microbiology laboratory is used for storing fungal culture at 4 ^{0}C. When cultures are stored at low temperature microorganisms are fairy inactive and will not suffer damage due to the evaporation of a medium. It is also used to store sterile media to prevent dehydration and to serve as a respiratory for antibiotics and biochemical reagent.

- **Release:** separation of inoculum from a reproductive structure.

- **Reproduction:** development of a new generation of pathogens.

- **Reproductive isolation:** barrier of sexual reproduction by geographical, physical or biological separation. Reproductive isolation is considered as a main driving force of speciation.

- **Resistance:** a host plant can be considered resistant if it has the ability to suppress or retard virus activity. Resistant is the opposite of susceptible and may be quantitatively identified as high (extreme), moderate or low, depending on the effectiveness of the protective mechanism.

- **Resolution:** Ability of an optical system to distinguish two adjacent points from one another

- **Resting spore:** A sexual or other thick-walled spore of a fungus that is resistant to extremes in temperature and moisture and which often germinates only after a period of time from its formation.

- **Restriction enzymes:** A group of enzymes from bacteria that break internal bonds of DNA at highly specific points.

- **Retention:** the length of time after virus acquisition that the vector remains viruliferous.

- **Retraction septa:** secondary or adventitious septa formed in elongating basidium.

- **RFLP:** Restriction pattern can be studied by highlighting certain bands by hybridization to a specific probe DNA and comparing the strains on the basis of RFLP (Restriction Fragment Length Polymorphism).

- **Rhamnolipids:** natural emulsifiers consisting of one or two molecules each of rhamnose and β-hydroxy fatty acids of varying length. They exhibit antibacterial and antifungal activity and are industrial candidates for assisting in the remediation of oil spills.

- **Rhizoid:** A short, thin hypha growing in a root-like fashion toward the substrate

  (or)

  Rhizoids: These are slender root like branched structures found in the substratum produced by some fungi which are useful for anchoring the thallus to substratum and for obtaining nourishment from the substrate.

- **Rhizomorphs:** Thick strands of somatic hyphae in which the hyphae loose their individuality and form complex tissues that are resistant to adverse conditions and remain dormant until favourable conditions return. The structure of growing tip of rhizomorphs resemble that of a root tip, hence the name rhizomorph

- **Rhizosphere colonizers**: Those organisms which colonize the dead substrates in the root region and continue to live like that for a longer period which are more tolerant to soil antagonism.

- **Rhizosphere effect:** effect of root secretions in the rhizosphere on microbial biomass, activity, and community composition as compared with the bulk soil.

- **Rhizosphere:** narrow zone immediately surrounding the root system that is influenced by root secretions and associated microbes.

- **Ribosomal frameshifting:** ribosomes switching reading frame on an mRNA, in response to the presence of a slippery site and/or a pseudoknot

- **Ring spot:** a circular area of chlorosis with a green center; a symptom of many virus diseases

- **RNA interference (RNAi):** a cellular mechanism that recognizes and regulates/degrades RNA in a sequence specific manner.

(or)

RNA interference (RNAi): RNAi is a cellular mechanism in which dsRNA triggers drive the posttranscriptional silencing of endogenous genes with homologous sequences.

- **RNA motif:** An ordered and stacked array of non-Watson- Crick base pairs folding into a distinct three-dimensional structure.

- **RNA recombination:** a major factor in virus evolution that can change plant virus populations, resulting in enhanced pathogenicity, extended host range, or overcoming host resistance factors.

- **RNAi lethal:** Silencing of some genes by RNAi leads to a lethal phenotype.

- **Root inhabitants**: These are more specialized parasites that survive in soils in close association with their hosts. The active saprophytic phase remains as long as the host tissue in which they are living as parasites is not completely decomposed

- **Rot:** the softening, discoloration, and disintegration of succulent plant tissue as the result of fungal or bacterial infection

- **Rouging**: Removal of diseased plants or their affected organs from field, which prevent the dissemination of plant pathogens.

- **Russet:** brownish roughened areas on skin of fruit as a result of cork formation

- **Rust:** a type of disease caused by a specific group of fungi, often producing orange-red "rust" colored spores.

- **Safeners:** A Chemical which reduces the phytotoxicity of another chemical is called safener.
- **Salicylic acid (SA):** plant hormone essential for the immune response against biotrophic pathogens.
- **Salmonellosis:** infection of the lining of the intestine with *Salmonelia* spp., often caused by food poisoning.
- **Sanitation:** Removing all old leaves and stems from beneath trees and shrubs eliminates most of the disease organisms on the soil surface. Many diseases reproduce in dead tissue on the soil surface.
- **Saprophyte:** An organism that uses dead organic material for food (or) Organisms which obtain nutrition on from dead organic matter either completely or for a part of their life. A large number of fungi fall under this category

- **Satellite virus:** virus always associated with helper viruses and depend on for multiplication and infection
- **Scab:** a roughened crust-like diseased area on the surface of a plant organ; a disease in which such areas form
- **Sclerotia:** The mycelium of some fungi becomes hard and forms reproductive structures known as sclerotia. These sclerotia or hard bodies will remain dormant in the soil for several years or until a susceptible crop is planted. *Sclerotiumrolfsii*, which causes crown rot of vegetables, is a good example of a fungus with this kind of reproduction.

(or)

Sclerotium: It is a hard, round (looks like mustard seed)/ cylindrical or elongated (*Claviceps*) dark coloured (black or brown) resting body formed due to aggregation of mycelium, the component hyphae loose their individuality , resistant to unfavorable conditions and remain dormant for a longer period of time and germinate on the return of favorable conditions. Eg. *Sclerotium, Rhizoctonia*.

- **Scorch**: burning of leaf margins as a result of infection or unfavorable environmental conditions

- **Secondary infection:** Any infection caused by inoculum produced as a result of a primary or a subsequent infection; an infection caused by secondary inoculum.

- **Secondary inoculum:** Inoculum produced by infections that take place during the same growing season.

- **Secondary metabolite**: a metabolite that is not part of the primary metabolic network of the cells. Primary metabolites are components of fundamental biochemicalpathways (e.g. glycolysis) that are present in all cells. Secondary metabolites only appear in cells that are specialized in some way e.g. in defense

- **Secretome:** all the proteins secreted by an organism.

- **Seed dip method:** Dipping the seed or seed materials in fungicidal solution for 5-20 minutes and drying them in shade before sowing. This method is particularly useful to check externally seed borne diseases.

- **Seed infection:** The seed in infected only when the pathogen has grown in or on it for some time and established its relationship with the seed tissues. Ex: Loose smut of wheat, where the fungus grows in the embryonic tissues and becomes dormant when the seed enters dormancy.

- **Seed treatment:** Seeds, tubers, bulbs, setts and other propagating materials are given physical / chemical treatment for eradication of pathogens present on them and for preventing their rot in the soil after planting.

- **Seedling dip / root dip:** The seedlings of vegetables and fruits are normally dipped in 0.25% copper oxychloride or 0.1% carbendazin solution for 5 minutes to protect against seedling blight and rots.

- **SEIDR:** SIR model with infected hosts separated into latent (E, i.e. exposed), cryptically infectious (I) and symptomatically infectious (D, i.e. detectable)/

- **SEIR-X:** SEIR model with a source of external inoculum (X).

- **Selection coefficient:** a measure of the extent to which natural selection acts to increase/reduce the contribution of a genotype to the next generation.

- **Selective media:** It is possible to isolate specific plant pathogens by using selective medium for that suitable selective medium has to be identified for different pathogens. Eg: King's B medium- *Pseudomonas* species, Nutrient agar medium – *Bacillus, Trichoderma* selective medium – *Trichoderma.*

- **Semi-persistent virus:** A virus which is retained for a few days by vectors. Virus do not pass to the progeny

- **Semi-solid medium:** Those medium which contains only half of the solidifying agent recommended for a solid medium

- **Semi-synthetic media:** Those media whose chemical composition is partially known. Any medium which contain agar they are called as semi-synthetic media. Eg: PDA medium and NA medium.

- **Semi-persistent transmission:** a mode of transmission requiring minutes to several hours for acquisition access and having a retention time of several hours to a few days.

- **Semi-persistent viruses:** plant viruses for which inoculativity by the vector is retained for a fewhours to a few days after acquisition from plants but vectors lose upon molting

- **Senescence:** cessation of inoculum production.

- **Septate hypha**: A hypha with septa or cross walls is called septate hypha

- **Septation in fungi:** Some fungal hyphae are provided with partitions or cross walls which divide the fungus into a number of compartments /cells. These cross walls are called septa

- **Serology:** The study of antigen-antibody interactions *in vitro*(or) A method using the specificity of the antigen–antibody reaction for the detection and identification of antigenic substances and the organisms that carry them.

- **Shot-hole:** a symptom in which small diseased fragments of leaves fall off and leave small holes in their place

- **Sibling species:** closely related species that are similar in appearance and other characteristics but are not capable of interbreeding.

- **Sign:** The pathogen or its parts or products seen on a host plant

- **Signal mimic:** a structural analogue of an acyl-HSL capable of affecting acyl-HSL-regulated behavior.

- **Signal molecules:** Host molecules that react to infection by a pathogen and transmit the signal to and activate proteins and genes in other parts of the cell and of the plant so they will produce the defense reaction.

- **Signal peptides:** amino acid sequences that direct the posttranslational targeting of proteins to the general secretory pathway.

- **Signaling genes:** Genes that respond to changes in the environment and set off signaling cascades that alter the expression of the genes of the organism.

- **Signaling pathways:** The series of compounds involved in the transmission of cellular signals, often involving several protein kinases functioning in series.

- **Silica gel:** A cooled spore suspension in 50% skimmed milk is poured on to free cooled silica gel in screw cap bottle and allowed to dry out room temperature and till the crystal separate (14 days) the caps screwed down and the bottle stored in refrigerator at 4-60°C.

- **Single site fungicide:** A fungicide that is active against only specific metabolic pathway or enzyme or protein needed by the fungus. e.g. Systemic fungicides

- **SIR:** classical formulation of epidemic model for susceptible (S), infected (I), removed (R) individuals.

- **Slurry treatment:** The seed is mixed with a dust fungicide in a special treater (Slurry treater) in which small calibrated amounts of concentrated liquid (about 5-20 ml/kg seed) are added, thus forming a soap-like slurry to ensure coating without undue wetting. This treatment is common in almost all seed processing plants owned by Government as well as private producers.

- **Soil drenching:** In this method fungicides are mixed in water and about the same Concentration as for spraying and applied to the soil surface either before or after plants emerge. The required quantity of fungicide suspension is applied with a sprinkler or rose can per unit area so that the fungicide reaches a depth of at least 10-15 cm.

- **Soil inhabitants**: Those organisms which survive indefinitely in the soil as saprophytes in the absence of the host plant

- **Soil solarization:** Attempt to reduce or eliminate pathogen populations in the soil by covering the soil with clear plastic so that sun rays will raise the soil temperature to levels that kill the pathogen.

(or)

Soil solarization: Soil solarization or slow soil pasteurization is the hydro/thermal soil heating accomplished by covering moist soil with polyethylene sheets as soil mulch during summer months for 4-6 weeks. Soil solarization was developed for the first time in Israel (Egley and Katan) for the management of plant pathogenic pests, diseases and weeds.

- **Soil sterilization:** Soil can be sterilized in green houses and sometimes in seed beds by aerated steam or hot water.

- **Solar treatment**: It is a safe and convenient method than hot water treatment. J.C. Luthra(1931) suggested this method for control of loose smut of wheat. Wheat seed is pre soaked in water for 4-5 h in the shade or in a room and then dried on ground/concrete floor in a thin layer in sun for 1 h usually at noon.

- **Solid Medium:** A solidifying or a gelling agent is commonly used for preparing semisolid (or) solid tissue culture medium.

- **Solidifying agents:** are used for preparing semisolid tissue culture media to enable explants to be placed in right contact with nutrient media (not submerged but on surface or slightly embedded) to provide aeration. Agar is high molecular weight polysaccharide obtained from sea weeds and can bind water. It is added to the medium in concentration ranging from 0.5% to 1 %(w/v).

- **Somaclonal variation:** genotypic or phenotypic variations occurring in tissue culture, the latter being either genetic or epigenetic in origin

(or)

Somaclonal variation: Variability in clones generated from a single mother plant, leaf, etc., by tissue culture.

- **Somatic embryogenesis:** embryo formation as a result of dedifferentiation of diploid cells.

- **Somatogamy:** Many higher fungi do not produce sex organs. In such cases somatogamy takes place.It is the union of 2 somatic hyphae or somatic cells representing opposite sexes to form sexual spores

- **Sorus:** Sorus in Greek means heap. ie., the spore bearing hyphae are grouped into small to large masses or clusters (eg) smut sori, rust sori.

- **Southern blot analysis:** Determines the integrity of the inserted gene: whether the gene is complete and not fragmented, at the correct orientation, and with one copy number. The DNA coding sequence is the probe binding to the single stranded genomic DNA of the transgenic plant which is implanted on a nitrocellulose paper. Autoradiography will reveal the transgenic status of the plant.

- **Spectrophotometer:** It is an electrically operated simple instrument used for estimating population of bacteria, based on the principle of turbidity determination. Turbidity is the cloudiness of the suspension. The more turbid a suspension, less light will be transmitted through it.

- **Spermatization**: Minute, uninucleate male cells called as spermatia which are produced on spermatiophores in a fruiting body (pycnium) are carried to female reproductive structures called receptive hyphae. Spermatia and receptive hyphae come in contact and contents of male spermatium migrate into female receptive hypha, thus making the cell binucleate. This process is called dikaryotization

- **Spiroplasma**: Spiroplasmas are helical, wall less prokaryotic microorganisms that are present in phloem of diseased plants, often helical in culture and are thought to be a kind of mycoplasma and can be cultured on artificial medium

- **Sporadic disease**: Occur at very irregular intervals and locations and in relatively fewer instances

- **Sporangiospores:** When the asexual spores are produced internally, within the sporangia,such spores are called sporangiospores

- **Spore:** It is a minute, simple propagating unit of the fungi, functioning as a seed but differs from it in lacking a preformed embryo that serves in the reproduction of same species.

- **Sporidia(-ium):** secondary spores formed by Tilletiales; in a broad sense used for any spore in the life cycle of smuts other than a teliospore.

- **Sporodochium :** A cushion shaped asexual fruiting body. Conidiophores arise from a central stroma and they are woven together on a mass of hyphae and produce conidia

(or)

Sporodochium: It is a fruiting body peculiar to the fungi *Fusarium* sp. It is a cushion shaped aggregation of hyphae which breaks through the host surface and bears conidiophore. These structures may also be formed in the mass of hyphae lying superficially over the substrate.

- **Spreading agent (Spreaders):** Spreaders are the materials added to establish improved contact between the spray materials and plant surface and thus ensuring a good coverage of fungicide. Wetting must precede spreading and this is the only distinction between wetting and spreading.

- **Sprinkle treatment**: The seed is sprinkled with a fungicidal liquid, solution or suspension, left damp with this for a definite period of tune and then dried. This method is widely used in countries like USA, Europe and UK.

- **Stage Micrometer:** It is a special glass slide having 0-100 divisions but in the centre having a known distance of 1mm. it 1mm is further divided into 1000 micrometer which is having uniform distance of 0.01mm or 10 micrometer between two divisions.

- **STAND:** Signal Transduction ATPases with Numerous Domains.

- **Sterilization** is a procedure used for elimination of microorganisms and maintaining aseptic (or) sterile conditions for successful culture of plant tissues (or) organs.

- **Stickers (Adhesives):** The materials which are added to spray or dust to improve the adherence to plant surfaces are called as stickers.

- **Stomata:** microscopic pores in the epidermis of aerial parts of a plant essential for gas exchange and water transpiration.

- **Strain/isolate/race:** taxonomic classifier for parasites below the species level. Strains/isolates/races are defined here by carrying different effector protein arsenals. Each strain/isolate/race is defined by its ability to colonize a unique set of accessions within a host species. In contrast to formaespeciales, members of different strains/isolates/races can co-occur and mate on the same host plant.

- **Strain-specific effector:** effector protein that is often recognized by a host NB-LRR protein. These effectors occur in a strain/isolate/race-specific manner and, together with the cognate (recognizing) NB-LRR proteins, are main drivers of the host–pathogen arms race. Historically, genes encoding strain-specific effector have been usually designated avirulence (AVR) genes.

- **Strategic decision:** decision aimed at optimizing a multicomponent approach to the management of a pest or pests, including the selection of the appropriate methods and decision rules for their most effective application.

- **Stroma**: It is a compact somatic structure looks like a mattress or a cushion on which or in which fructifications (spores or fruiting bodies) are usually formed

- **Stylet borne virus:** virus is thought to be transmitted by styletswithout entering insect

- **Stylets:** needleshaped mouthparts of insects, mites, and nematodes.
- **Sub culture**: Aseptic transfer of a part of a culture to a fresh medium Suspension culture : Culturing of cells (or) cell aggregates in liquid medium
- **Sub stomatalstroma:** cushion like structure formed below epidermis in sub stomatal region from which sporophores are produced
- **Suppressive soils:** Soils in which certain diseases are suppressed because of the presence in the soil of microorganisms antagonistic to the pathogen.
- **Suppressors:** pathogen products that suppress a resistance response of host plants by interfering with recognition or subsequent resistance gene expression by host plants.
- **Survival during dormancy:** persistence of pathogen during a period of adverse conditions.
- **Survival of inoculum during dispersal:** persistence of during dispersal.

- **Susceptibility**: The inability of a plant to resist the effect of a pathogen or other damaging factor.
- **Symbionin:** protein homolog of the *Escherichia coli* chaperone Gro EL that is secreted by aphid endosymbiotic bacteria.
- **Symbiosis:** an interaction between two organisms living together in a more or less intimate association.

(or)

Symbiosis: Some fungi derive nutrition from a living member to which they also provide some kind of benefit in return. This kind of relationship is termed as symbiosis (eg) VAM.

- **Sympatric speciation:** the formation of two or more descendant species from a single ancestral species all occupying the same geographic location.
- **Symplastic movement**: Movement of foliar fungicides along with photosynthates and sugars in phloem (It is downward movement)

Eg.: Metalaxyl, Foestyl-Al, Triadimefon

- **Symptom:** The external or internal reactions or alterations of a plant as a result of a disease.

- **Syncytium:** the system of highly modified host cells from which the cyst nematode feeds within the plant root.

- **Syndrome:** The set of varying symptoms characterizing a disease are collectively called a syndrome

- **Synergism:** It means the ability of two kinds of organisms to grow better or produce greater effect conjointly than either one could alone (eg) *Diplodianatelensis*and *Colletotrichumgleosporioides*together produce much greater effect on citrus bark than either one of the pair alone can produce.

(or)

Synergism: The concurrent parasitism of a host by two pathogens in which the symptoms or other effects produced are of greater magnitude than the sum of the effects of each pathogen acting alone.

- **Synnema:** It is nothing but the loose aggregation of erect conidiophore so as to form a dense fasicle, similar to mycelial strand. It may split in different ways near the apex, sometimes resembling a feather duster. Such arrangement is called as *coremium*and the +conidia are produced at its apex (eg) *Ceratocystis*sp, *Graphium*sp.

- **Synnemata:** (pl.synnema) A group of conidiophores often united at the base and free at the top. Conidia may be formed at its tip or along the length of synnema, resembling a long handled feather duster

- **Synthetic media:**They are those whose chemical composition is completely known. They are costly and take more time for preparation.

- **Systemic acquired resistance (SAR):** enhanced defensive capacity of the entire plant against a broad spectrum of pathogens;

acquired upon local induction by a pathogen

(or)

Systemic acquired resistance (SAR): the phenomenon that plants acquire an enhanced defensive capacity against subsequent pathogen attack as a result of a primary, limited infection.

- **Systemic infection:** The growth of pathogen from the point of entry to varying extents without showing adverse effect on tissues through which it passes

- **T** $= 2$ **symmetry:** the so-called forbidden triangulation symmetry, in which 120 chemically identical protein monomers, form 60 identical, asymmetric dimers arranged with icosahedral symmetry.

- **Tactical decision:** decision pertaining to methods to solve a given pest problem or details of how a chosen method should be applied.

- **Target:** the nucleic acid extracted from the test material or a transcript copy thereof, which issubsequently labeled and applied by hybridization to a microarray.

- **T-DNA:** Transferred DNA, the segment of the *Agroacterium* T_i plasmid which is transferred to the plant cell

- **Teichoic acid:** It is a water soluble polymer containing 30 or more repeat units of ribitol or glycerol phosphate residues joined through phosphodiester linkages

- **Teleomorph:** sexual ("perfect") form of an ascomycete or basidiomycete fungal pathogen (characterized by the presence of ascospores or basidiospores).

- **Temperate phage:** Phage which can establish lysogenic relation with susceptible bacteria (cf. virulent phage)

- **Test tube:** A test tube also known as a culture tube, is a common piece

of laboratory glassware consisting of a finger like length of glass or clear plastic tubing, open at the top, usually with a round U shaped bottom.

- **Tetraloop:** A type of four-base hairpin motif that often caps double helices in an RNA secondary structure.

- **Thallus:** Commonly called as vegetative body or fungal body. A thallus is a simple, entire body of the fungus devoid of chlorophyll with no differentiation into stem, roots and leaves lacking vascular system. the pathogen

- **Thaumatin:** a sweet protein from the fruit of the African shrub *Thaumatococcusdaniellii.*

- **Therapy** means cure of a disease, in which fungicide is applied after the pathogen is in contact with the host. Chemicals used are called therapeutants.There are regulations controlling the amount of some mycotoxins such as aflatoxin and ochratoxin permitted in food.

- **Thermal inactivation point:**the lowest temperature at which heating for a limited period (10 min), is sufficient to cause loss of virus infectivity.

- **Threatening pathogen:** invasive or indigenous pathogen able to cause significant crop losses in yield or quality, resulting in negative health, economic, and/or social consequences.

- **Tinsel**: It is a feathery structure consisting of a long rachis with lateral hair like projections called mastigonemes or flimmers on all sides along its entire length.

- **Tip blight:** death of shoot tips

- **TIR:** protein domain with homology to the *Drosophila* Toll and human Interleukin-1 receptor

- **TIR1:** the F-box protein subunit of the ubiquitin ligase complex SCFTIR1 and the auxin receptor promoting the degradation of Aux/IAA proteins.

- **TNL:** TIR-NB-LRR protein, an R protein containing a central NB-ARC domain fused to an N-terminal TIR domain and a C-terminal LRR domain.

- **Tolerance:** a host response to virus infection that results in negligible or mild symptom expression, but relatively normal levels of virus concentration and movement within the host compared with a susceptible host

- **Toxicity:** The capacity of a compound to produce injury.

- **Toxin:** A compound produced by a microorganism; being toxic to a plant or animal.

  (or)

  Toxins: pathogen molecules that cause plant cell death thereby facilitating colonization by necrotrophic pathogens

- **Transcapsidation:** the encapsulation of the nucleic acid of one virus strain with the protein of another, during simultaneous infection and replication of two strains.

- **Transmission rate:** the rate at which the pathogen is transmitted from infectious to healthy hosts.

- **Transmission:** The transfer or spread of a virus or other pathogen from one plant to another.

- **Transovarial transmission:** transmission of viruses from female parent to offspring through the ovaries.

- **Transport:** movement of inoculum from one location to another.

- **Transposable element:** A segment of chromosomal DNA that can move around (transpose) in the genome and integrate at different sites on the chromosomes.

- **True vascular wilt:** a disease in which the pathogen moves systemically throughout the host in the nonliving vessels without directly attacking parenchyma cells during the early stages of disease.

- **Tumor:** a malignant overgrowth of tissue (or) an uncontrolled overgrowth of tissue.
- **Tyloses:** Tyloses are the overgrowths of the protoplast of adjacent living parenchymatous cells, which protrude into xylem vessels through pits.
- **Type III/VI secretion system (T3SS/T6SS):** consists of distinct protein composition and is responsible for injection of effectors and toxins into host cells.
- **U**niflagellate zoospore : A zoospore with a single flagellum, may be placed at anterior or posterior end of spore
- **Unitunicateascus:** The ascus wall consists of 2 layers which are rigid and unite together throughout length and existence of the ascus. . The outer wall is called exotunica or exoascus and the inner wall is called endotunica or endoascus and not separated during spore release.

The spores are released through a terminal pore, slit or operculum

- **Universal primers:** PCR primers designed to conserve sequence and used to amplify DNA from multiple different organisms.
- **Uv light:** Used for killing the microorganisms. It can be used 10-20 min before starting the work.
- **V**ariability: The property or ability of an organism to change its characteristics from one generation to the other.
- **V-ATPase:** a multisubunit proton pump that transports H+ across plasma membranes while hydrolyzing ATP.
- **Vector resistance:** resistance of a host plant to the vector of a virus.
- **Vector:** an organism that transmits a virus from an infected to a healthy host by a mechanism that is governed by specific features of virus, vector, and host.
- **Vegetative incompatibility:** a genetically controlled self/nonself

recognition system in fungi that determines the ability to undergo hyphal anastomosis.

(or)

Vegetative incompatibility: Failure of the hyphae of strains of the same species of a fungus to fuse and form anastomoses.

- **Vein banding:** retention of bands of green tissue along the veins while the tissue between veins has become chlorotic

(or)

Vein clearing: destruction of chlorophyll adjacent or in the vein tissue as a result of infection by a virus or other pathogen

- **Vertical resistance**: When a variety is more resistant to some races of the pathogen than others, the resistance is called vertical resistance (race-specific resistance, qualitative resistance, discriminatory resistance). Vertical resistance is usually governed by single gene and is unstable.

- **Vesicle:** A bubble-like structure produced by a zoosporangium in which zoospores are released or are differentiated.

- **Vessel:** A xylem element or series of such elements whose function is to conduct water and mineral nutrients.

- **Viral suppressor:** viral-encoded molecules that modulate host RNAi defense mechanisms.

- **Virion:** the complete virus particle consisting of the nucleic acid and protein shell.

- **Viroids**: Small, low molecular weight ribonucleic acids(RNA) that can infect plant cells, replicate themselves and cause disease in plants

- **Virulence genes:** Enable a pathogen to express increased virulence on only one or a few related hosts.

- **Virulence:** for nematodes, this refers to the ability to develop on a resistant host plant, and does not include a concept of amount of disease induced.

- **Viruliferous:** a vector that carries or contains virus.

- **Virus:** A sub-microscopic, obligate parasite consisting of nucleic acid and protein that multiplies only intracellularly and is potentially pathogenic

- **Virus-induced gene silencing (VIGS):** a gene transcript suppression technique to identify plant gene function. A chimeric plant virus, containing a fragment of a plant gene, is used to infect a plant. As part of the antiviral response, mRNAs from the endogenous plant gene are specifically degraded.

- **Virusoid:** The extra-small circular RNA component of some isometric RNA viruses.

- **W**ash glasses: It is used for holding small samples or for covering beakers.

- **Water bath:** It is an insulated metallic box fitted with an electric heating mechanism and a thermostat, which maintains the temperature at desired level. There are racks for holding test tubes. These are usually used for melting of media, testing enzymatic activities of various microorganisms, widal test etc.

- **Western blot analysis:** It is an analytical technique used to detect whether the transgenic plants produce the specific protein product of the introduced gene. Protein samples are extracted from the transgenic plants, processed into denatured proteins and transferred to a nitrocellulose membrane. The protein is then probed or detected using the antibodies specific to the target protein.

- **Wettable Powders (WP):** Wettable powder is a very common formulation for most of the fungicides, which is used for spray mixtures. The modern wettable

powders are water-dispersible which have the quality to wet easily and disperse well in water. They are also called as Water-Dispersible Powders (WDP).

- **Wetting agent (Wetters):** These are the materials which are added to ensure that there will be no layer of air between a solid and a liquid as they reduce the surface tension of the particles. Wetting agents, when added to aqueous fungicidal preparation, help in easy deposition on leaves. Eg. Polyethylene oxide condensate, esters of fatty acids and flour.

- **Whiplash:** A flagellum with long, thick, rigid basal portion and with a short, narrow, flexible, upper portion .It gives a whip like appearance to flagellum.

- **Wilt:** loss of rigidity and drooping of plant parts generally caused by insufficient water in the Plant

- **Witches' broom:** broom-like growth or massed proliferation caused by the dense clustering of branches in woody plants

- **Y**ellows: a group of systemic mycoplasma-caused diseases often resulting in wilt, witches broom, or decline

- **Yield loss:** decrease in quantitative output of a crop resulting from the injury caused by a pathogen (or more generally, a pest), or from injuries caused by several pathogens (or pests).

- **Z**oonotic: a disease that can be transmitted from animals to humans.

- **Zoospores / planospores:** sporangiospores which are motile by flagella are called zoospores.Also known as planospores.Eg. *Pythium, Phytophthora.*

- **Zygomycotina:** Thallus is aseptate mycelium. Motile spores are absent. Asexual spores are sporangiospores

(aplanospores).Sexual spores are zygospores. Sexual reproduction through gametangial copulation.

- **Zygospore**: A thick walled sexual resting spore produced by the fusion of two morphologically similar gametangia

- **β-1,3-glucanases:** enzymes that hydrolyze β-1,3 glycosidic bonds in linear or branched glucans

DISEASES OF FIELD CROPS

RICE

- **Blast**: *Pyricularia oryzae (Syn: P. grisea) (Sexual stage: Magnaporthe grisea)*

- **Brown Spot:** *Bipolaris oryzae* (Syn: *Helminthosporium oryzae*) (Sexual stage: *Cochliobolus miyabeanus*)

- **Sheath rot:** *Sarocladium oryzae* (Syn: *Acrocylindrium oryzae*)

- **Stem rot:** *Sclerotium oryzae* (Sexual stage: *Leptosphaeria salvinii*)

- **Narrow brown leaf spot:** *Cercospora oryzae* (Sexual stage: *Sphaerulina oryzae*)

- **Sheath blight:** *Rhizoctonia solani* (Sexual stage : *Thanetophorus cucumeris*)

- **False smut:** *Ustilaginoidea virens* (P.S: *Claviceps oryzae - sativa*)

- **Bacterial leaf blight:** *Xanthomonas oryzae pv. oryzae*

- **Bacterial leaf streak:** *Xanthomonas campestris p.v. oryzicola*

- **Tungro disease:** Rice Tungro Virus (RTV)

WHEAT

- **Black or stem rust:** *Puccinia graminis tritici*

- **Leaf, brown or orange rust:** *Puccinia recondite*

- **Yellow or stripe rust:** *Puccinia striformis*

- **Loose smut:** *Ustilago nuda tritici*

- **Karnal bunt:** *Neovossia indica* (*Tilletia indica*)

- **Leaf blight:** *Alternaria triticina*

- **Tundu disease or yellow slime disease:** *Anguina tritici (Nematode)* + *Corynebacterium tritici* or *Clavibacter tritici*

SORGHUM

- **Anthracnose or red leaf spot:** *Colletotrichum graminicola*
- **Rust:** *Puccinia purpurea*
- **Ergot or Sugary disease:** *Claviceps sorghi* or *Sphacelia sorghi*
- **Head mould/Grain mould/ Head blight:** (*Fusarium semitectum*, *F.moniliforme*, *Curvularia lunata*, *Alternaria* spp., *Aspergillus* spp., *Cheatomium* spp., *Rhizopus* spp., *Helminthosporium* spp. and *Phoma* spp.)
- **Leaf blight or leaf stripe:** *Exserohilum turcicum* or *Trichometasphaeria turcica* (Syn : *Helminthosporium turcicum* or *Drechslera turcicum*)

- **Grain smut/Kernel smut/ Covered smut / Short smut:** *Sphacelotheca sorghi* or *Sporisorium sorghi*
- **Charcoal rot or hollow stem or Stalk rot blight:** *Macrophomina phaseolina*
- **Downy Mildew or Leaf shredding:** *Peronosclerospora sorghi*

MAIZE

- **Turcicum Leaf blight:** *Helminthosporium turcicum (Syn : H. maydis)*
- **Post flowering stalk rot/*Cephalosporium* wilt (Black bundle disease and late wilt):** *Cephalosporium acremonium/ Cephalosporium maydis*
- **Charcoal rot:** *Macrophomina phaseolina (Sclerotial stage: Rhizoctonia bataticola)*
- **Banded leaf and sheath blight:** *Rhizoctonia solani* (Perfect stage: *Thanetophorus sasakii*)

- **Downy mildew:** Crazy top DM – *Sclerophthora macrospora*

BAJRA/CUMBU/PREARL MILLET

- **Downy mildew or Green ear:** *Sclerospora graminicola*
- **Rust:** *Puccinia penniseti*
- **Ergot or Sugary disease:** *Claviceps fusiformis or C. microcephala*
- **Smut:** *Tolyposporium penicillariae*

RAGI/FINGER MILLET

- **Blast:** *Pyricularia grisea*
- **Smut:** *Melanopsichium eleusinis*
- **Mosaic:** *Sugarcane mosaic virus*

RED GRAM

- **Phytophthora blight / Stem blight:** *Phytophthora drechsleri f. sp. cajani*
- **Wilt:** *Fusarium oxysporum f. sp. udum*
- **Sterility Mosaic:** *Sterility mosaic virus*

- **Bacterial leaf spot and stem canker:** *Xanthomonas campestris pv. Cajani*

BENGAL GRAM

- **Wilt:** *Fusarium oxysporum f.sp. cicero*
- **Rust:** *Uromyces ciceris-arietini*
- ***Ascochyta blight:*** *Ascochyta rabiei (Perfect stage: Mycosphaerella pinodes)*
- **Stem and Root rot or dry root rot:** *Rhizoctonia bataticola (Pycnidial stage: Macrophomina phaseolina) (Sexual stage: Thanatephorus cucumeris)*

BLACK GREEM/GREEN GRAM

- **Powdery mildew:** *Erysiphe polygoni*
- **Rust:** *Uromyces phaseoli typical* (Syn: *U.appendiculatus*)
- **Cercospora leaf spot:** *Cercospora canescens*
- **Corynespora leaf spot:** *Corynespora cassicola*

- **Angular black spot:** *Protomycopsis phaseoli or P. patelii (Syn: Erratomyces patelii)*
- **Dry root rot:** *Rhizoctonia bataticola* (Pycnidial stage : *Macrophomina phaseolina*)
- **Bacterial leaf spot:** *Xanthomonas phaseoli*
- **Yellow mosaic:** *Mungbean yellow mosaic virus*
- **Leaf crinkle:** *Leaf crinkle virus*

SOYBEAN

- **Rust:** *Phakopsora pachyrhizi*
- **Soybean mosaic:** *Soybean mosaic virus*
- **Bacterial pustule:** *Xanthomonas axonopodis pv. Glycines*

COWPEA

- **Cowpea mosaic:** *Cowpea yellow mosaic virus (Syn: Cowpea mosaic virus, yellow strain)*

GROUNDNUT

- **Early leaf spot:** *Cercospora arachidicola* **(Sexual Stage):** *Mycosphaerella arachidis*
- **Late leaf spot:** *Phaeoisariopsis personata* (Sexual stage: *Mycosphaerella berkeleyii*) (Syn: *Cercosporidium personatum*)
- **Rust:** *Puccinia arachidis*
- **Pepper leaf spot or leaf scorch:** *Leptosphaerulina crassiasca*
- **Stem rot:** *Sclerotium rolfsii*
- **Bud necrosis or Peanut spotted wilt or groundnut ring mosaic:** *Tomato spotted wilt virus (TSWV-Tospovirus)*
- **Peanut Stem necrosis disease (PSND):** *Tobacco streak virus (Ilarvirus)*

GINGELLY

- **Alternaria leaf spot:** *Alternaria sesame*

- **Powdery mildew:** *Leveillula taurica* or *Erysiphe cichoracearum* (Conidial stage: *Oidiopsis taurica* or *Oidium acanthosperma*)
- **Phyllody:** *Phytoplasma*
- **Root rot or stem rot or charcoal rot:** *Macrophomina phaseolina,* (Sclerotial stage: *Rhizoctonia bataticola*)
- **Bacterial leaf spot:** *Pseudomonas sasami* or *Ralstonia syringae pv. Sesame*

SUNFLOWER

- **Leaf blight:** *Alternaria helianthi*
- **Rust:** *Puccinia helianthi*
- **Powdery mildew:** *Erysiphe cichoracearum*
- **Head rot:** *Rhizopus sp. (*Mostly *R. arrhizus)*
- **Sclerotial wilt/Collar rot:** *Sclerotium rolfsii*
- **Downy mildew:** *Plasmopara halstedii*
- **Mosaic:** *Virus*
- **Sunflower necrosis virus (SND):** *Tobacco streak virus*

SAFFLOWER

- **Leaf blight:** *Alternaria carthami*
- **Wilt:** *Fusarium oxysporum f.sp. carthami*
- **Rust:** *Puccinia carthami (Puccinia calcitrapae var. centaureae) or P. verruca or Aecidium carthami*
- **Mosaic:** *Cucumber mosaic virus (CMV)*

MUSTARD

- **White rust:** *Albugo candida or A. cruciferarum*
- **Downy mildew:** *Peronospora parasitica*
- **Powdery mildew:** *Erysiphe cruciferarum*
- **Alternaria leaf spot:** *Alternaria brassicae* and *A. brassicola*

CASTOR

- **Wilt:** *Fusarium oxysporum f.sp. ricini*
- **Root rot/Charcoal rot:** *Macrophomina phaseolina*
- **Bacterial leaf spot:** *Xanthomonas campestris pv. ricini*

- **Seedling blight:** *Phytophthora parasitica*
- **Rust:** *Melampsora ricini*

COTTON

- **Bacterial blight or Angular leaf spot or Black arm:** *Xanthomonas campestris* pv. *malvacearum*
- **Fusarium wilt:** *Fusarium oxysporum* f.sp. *vasinfectum*
- **Verticillium wilt:** *Verticillium dahlia*
- **Root rot:** *Rhizoctonia bataticola* (*Pycnidial stage: Macrophomina phaseolina*)
- **Grey or Areolate mildew:** *Ramularia areola* (Sexual stage: *Mycosphaerella areola*)
- **Anthracnose:** *Colletotrichum capsici*
- ***Alternaria* leaf spot:** *Alternaria macrospora*
- ***Cercospora* Leaf spot:** *Cercospora gossypina*
- ***Helminthosporium* Leaf spot:** *Helminthosporium gossypii*

- **Rust:** *Phakopsora gossypii* (Tropical rust), *Puccinia cacabata* (South western rust), *Puccinia schedonnardi* (Cotton rust-USA)

SUGARCANE

- **Red rot:** *Colletotrichum falcatum* (Sexual stage: *Physalospora tucumanensis* or *Glomerella tucumanensis*)
- **Whip Smut:** *Ustilago scitaminea*
- **Wilt:** *Cephalosporium sacchari*
- **Ring spot:** *Leptosphaeria sacchari*
- **Grassy shoo:** *Phytoplasma*
- **Mosaic:** *Sugarcane Mosaic Virus*
- **Ratoon stunting:** *Clavibacter xyli* pv. *xyli* (*Xylem limited fastidious bacteria*)
- **Rust:** *P. melanocephala, P. kuehnii (Syn: Puccinia erianthi)*

TOBACCO

- **Black shank:** *Phytophthora parasitica* var. *nicotianae*
- **Damping off:** *Pythium aphanidermatum*

- **Frog eye spot:** *Cercospora nicotianae*
- **Brown spot:** *Alternaria alternata*
- **Mosaic:** *Tobacco Mosaic Virus (TMV) or Nicotiana virus I*
- **Leaf curl:** *Tobacco leaf curl virus or Nicotiana Virus 10 (Ruga tabaci)*

BETELVINE

- **Root and stem rot:** *(Phytophthora parasitica, Sclerotium rolfsii and Fusarium solani)*
- **Anthracnose/Leaf spot/Marginal blight:** *Colletotrichum capsici*

DISEASES OF VEGETABLES

POTATO

- **Late blight :** *Phytopthora infestans*
- **Early blight:** *Alternaria solani*
- **Black scurf and stem canker:** *Rhizoctonia solani*
- **Dry rots:** *Fusarium* spp.

- **Bacterial wilt:** *Pseudomonas solanacearum*
- **Soft rot and black leg:** *Erwinia carotovora*
- **Common scab:** *Streptomyces scabies*
- **Leaf roll:** Virus (vector - Myzus persicae)
- **Purple top roll:** Phytoplasma
- **Severe mosaic :** Virus (vector - *Myzus persicae*)
- **Wart :** *Synchytrium endobioticum*
- **Powdery scab:** *Spongospora subterranea.*

BRINJAL

- **Damping off:** *Pythium* spp.
- **Early blight:** *Alternaria solani*
- **Late blight:** *Phytophthora infestans*
- **Buck eye rot of tomato:** *Phytophthora nicotianae* var. *parasitica*
- **Wilt:** *Fusarium oxysporum* f. sp. *lycopersici*
- **Bacterial wilt:** *Pseudomons solanacearum var. abiaticum*

- **Mosaic:** Tobacco mosaic virus
- **Leaf curl:** Tobacco leaf curl virus
- **Tomato spotted wilt virus:** *Tomato spotted with virus (TSWV)*

BRINJAL

- **Damping off:** *Pythium aphanidermatum P. debaryanum P. ultimum*
- **Phomopsis blight and Fruit rot:** *Phomopsis vexans*
- **Bacterial wilt:** *Pseudomonas solanacearum*
- **Leaf spots:** *Cercospora melongenae*
- ***Alternaria* leaf spot:** *Alternaria melongenae*
- **Little leaf :** Phytoplasma

BHENDI

- **Yellow vein mosaic:** Virus
- **Powdery mildew:** *Erysiphe cichoracearum*
- **Damping off:** *Pythium indicum*

- ***Cercospora* leaf spot :** *Cercospora abelmoschi*

TAPIOCA (CASSAVA)

- **Tapioca mosaic :** Virus
- ***Cercospora* leaf spot :** *Cercospora henningsii*

ONION

- **Purple blotch :** *Alternarja porri*
- **Smut:** *Urocystis cepulae*
- **Basal rot:** *Fusarium oxysporum f.sp.cepae*
- **Purple blotch:** *Alternarja porri*

CUCURBITS

- **Powdery mildew:** *Erysiphe cichoracearum*
- **Downy mildew:** *Pseudoperonospora cubensis*
- **Anthracnose:** *Colletotrichum lagenarium*
- **Leaf spot :** *Cercospora*

CRUCIFEROUS

- **Club root :** *Plosmodiophora brassicae*
- **Ring spot:** *Mycosphaerella brassicola*
- **Downy mildew:** *Peronospora parasitica*
- **Black rot:** *Xanthomonas oxonopodis* pv. oxonopodis
- **Leaf spot:** *Alternaria brassicicola; A. brassicae.*
- **Head rot:** *Sclerotinia sclerotiorum*
- **White rust of Crucifers :** *Albugo candida (Cystopus candidus)*

BEANS

- **Anthracnose:** *Colletotrichum lindemuthianum*
- **Rust:** *Uromyces phaseoli typica, Uromyces appendiculatus*
- **Yellow mosaic:** Bean Yellow Mosaic Virus, Mungbean yellow mosaic virus or Phaseolus virus - 2 (Geminivirus: ss DNA)

- **Common bean mosaic virus/ Green mosaic:** *Bean common mosaic virus* (Potyvirus with long flexuous rods having ssRNA)

DISEASES OF FRUIT CROPS

MANGO

- **Powdery mildew:** *Oidium mangiferae (Perfect stage: Eyrsiphe polygoni)*
- **Anthracnose:** *Colletotrichum gloeosporioides (PS: Glomerella cingulata)*
- **Mango Malformation**: *Fusarium moliliforme var. subglutinans*
- **Sooty mould**: *Capnodium ramosum*
- **Red rust:** *Cephaleuros virescens* (algae)

BANANA

- **Yellow Sigatoka :** *Mycosphaerella musicola (I.S: Pseudocercospora musae)*

- **Black sigatoka**: *Mycosphaerella fijiensis (I.S: Paracercospora fijiensis)*
- **Panama wilt**: *Fusarium oxysporum f.sp. cubense*
- **Moko disease / Bacterial wilt**: *Ralstonia solanacearum (race 2) (Pseudomonas or Burkholderia)*
- ***Erwinia* rhizome rot**: *Erwinia caratovora* sub.sp. *caratovora* and *Erwinia chrysanthemii*
- **Bunchy top/Curly top/ cabbage top/Strangles disease**: Banana bunchy top virus (BBTV)
- **Banana Mosaic/Infectious chlorosis/Heart rot:**Cucumber Mosaic Virus (CMV)
- **Banana bract mosaic**: *Banana bract mosaic virus* (BBrMV)

GRAPE

- **Powdery mildew**: *Uncinula necator (I.S: Oidium tuckeri)*
- **Downy mildew**: *Plasmopara viticola*

- **Anthracnose or Birds eye disease**: *Elsinoe ampelina* (I.S: *Gloeosporium ampelophagum* or *Sphaceloma ampelina*)
- **Alternaria leaf spot**: *Alternaria vitis*
- **Rust**: *Phakopsora euvitis*

CITRUS

- **Gummosis**: *Phytophthora nicotianae* var. *parasitica, P. palmivora, P. citrophthora*
- **Diplodia gummosis**: *Diplodia natalensis* (Perfect stage: *Physalospora rhodina*)
- **Dry root rot**: *Fusarium solani*
- **Citrus canker**: *Xanthomonas axonopodis* pv. *citri*
- **Tristeza or quick decline**: Citrus Tristeza Virus (CTV)\
- **Greening or Huanglongbin (HLB)**: *Candidatus Liberobacter asiaticus* (Fastidious Phloem
- limited Bacterium)
- **Felt disease**: *Septobasidium pseudopedicellatum*

APPLE

- **Scab:** *Venturia inaequalis (I. S: Spilocaea pomi)*
- **Powdery mildew:** *Podosphaera leucotricha* (I. S: *Oidium* spp)
- **Fire blight of apple:** *Venturia ineuqalis*
- **Crown gall:** *Agrobacterium tumefaciens*

PINEAPPLE

- **Black-rot / Soft rot:** *Chalara paradoxa*
- **Heart-rot:** *Phytophthora parasitica*
- **Leaf and Fruit-rot:** *Cyratostomella paradoxa*
- **Leaf Spot:** *Phytophthora* sp.
- **Thielaviopsis rot:** *Thielaviopsis paradoxa*

GUAVA

- **Wilt:** *Fusaium oxysporum f.sp. psidii, F. solani*
- **Anthracnose:** *Gloesporium psidii, Glomerella psidii*

- ***Cercospora Leaf Spot****: Cercospora sawadae*
- **Scab:** *Pestalotia psidii*

SAPOTA

- **Leaf spot :** *Phleopheospora indica*
- **Base rot:** *Ceratocystis paradoxa*
- **Heart rot:** *Phytophthora parasitica*
- **Anthracnose:** *Colletotrichum gloeosporioides*
- **Sooty Mould:** *Capnodium* sp.
- **Flat Leaf or Fasciation:** *Botrydiplodia theobromae*

PAPAYA

- **Foot rot or Stem rot:** *Pythium aphanidermatum*
- **Mosaic:** *Papaya mosaic virus* or *Papaya ringspot virus* or *Carica virus* 1
- **Leaf curl:** *Tobacco leaf curl virus* or *Nicotiana virus* 10
- **Anthracnose:** *Colletotrichum papaya*

POMEGRANATE

- **Anthracnose:** *Colletotrichum gloeosporioides*
- **Bacterial leaf spot:** *Xanthomonas axonopodis* pv. *punicae*

BER

- **Powdery mildew:** *Oidium erysiphoides f.sp. zizyphi*

MULBERRY

- **Powdery mildew:** *Phyllactinia corylea, P. guttata, P. suffulata (IS: Ovulariopsis corylea)*

DISEASES OF PLANTATION CROPS

COCONUT

- **Tanjore wilt/ Basal stem end rot/ Ganoderma wilt:** *Ganoderma lucidem and Ganoderma applanatum*
- **Bud rot:** *Phytophthora palmivora*

- **Leaf blight:** *Lasiodiplodia theobromae*
- **Stem bleeding disease:** *Thielaviopsis paradoxa*
- **Root wilt (or) Kerala wilt disease:** *Phytoplasma*
- **Leaf rot disease:** *Colletotrichum gloeosporioides, Exserohilum rostratum* and *Fusarium* spp.

ARECANUT

- **Foot rot or Anabe roga:** *Ganoderma lucidum*
- **Yellow leaf disease:** *Phytoplasma*
- **Mahali / kolerogo/ fruit rot:** *Phytophthora arecae*
- **Bud rot:** *Phytophthora arecae*
- **Inflorescence die back and button shedding:** *Colletotrichum gloeosporioides*

TEA

- **Algal leaf spot/ red rust:** *Cephaleuros virescens*
- **Brown blight, grey blight:** *Colletotrichum* sp., *Pestalotiopsis* sp.
- **Blister blight:** *Exobasidium vexans*
- **Horse hair blight:** *Marasmius crinisequi*
- **Twig dieback, stem canker:** *Macrophoma theicola*
- **Black root rot:** *Rosellina arcuata*

COFFEE

- **Rust:** *Hemileia vastatrix*
- **Brown leaf spot:** *Cercospora coffeicola*
- **Damping off/Collar rot:** *Rhizocotonia solani*
- **Die back or Anthranos:** *Collectorichum coffeasum*
- **Black rot or koleroga:** *Corticium salmonicolor*
- **Root rot:** *Fusarium* spp.

- **Berry blotch:** *Cercospora coffeicola*

RUBBER

- **Abnormal leaf fall:** *Phytophthora palmivora & P. nicotianae var. parasitica*
- **Birds eye spot:** *Drechslera heveae (Helminthosporium heveae)*
- **Corynespora leaf spot:** *Corynespora cossicola*
- **Pink disease:** *Corticium salminicolor*
- **Powdery mildew:** *Oidium heveae*
- **Brown root disease:** *Fomes noxius*
- ***Colletotrichum* Leaf Disease:** *Colletotrichum acutatum* and *Colletotrichum gloeosporioides*

COCOA

- **Seedling blight:** *Phytophthora palmivora*
- **Black Pod rot:** *Phytophthora palmivora, P. megakarya, P. citrophthora* and *P. capsici*

- **Stem Canker:** *Phytophthora palmivora*
- **Vascular Streak Dieback (VSD):** *Oncobasidium theobromae*
- **Cherelle Rot:** *Colletotrichum gloeosporioides*

DISEASES OF MEDICINAL PLANTS

ASHWAGANDHA

- **Leaf spot:** *Alternaria dianthicola*
- **Root rot and wilt:** *Fusarium solani*
- **Leaf curl:** *Tobacco leaf curl virus*

BELLADONNA

- **Leaf spot:** *Ascochyta atropae*
- **Collar rot:** *Rhizoctonia solani*
- **Roots-rot:** *Pythium butleri*
- **Belladonna mosaic:** Belladonna mosaic virus
- **Belladonna mottle:** Belladonna mottle virus

CINCHONA

- **Seedling Blight:** *Phytophthora palmivora*
- **Die - back:** *Phytophthora parasitica*
- **Pink - disease:** *Corticium salmonicolor*
- **Damping-off:** *Pythium vexans*

COLEUS

- **Downy mildew:** *Peronospora lamii*
- **Damping-off:** *Pythium aphanidermatum*
- **Leaf spot:** *Alternaria* sp.
- **Root - knot nematode:** *Meloidogyne incognita*
- **Wilt and root rot:** *Macrophomina phaseolina, Sclerotium rolfsii, Fusarium* sp. and *Meloidogyne incognita*
- **Botrytis blight:** *Botrytis cinerea*
- ***Corynespora* leaf spot:** *Corynespora cassicola*

DIGITALIS

- **Anthracnose:** *Colletotrichum fuscum*
- **Leaf spot:** *Septoria digitalis* and *Phyllosticta digitalis*

DIOSCOREA

- **Rust:** *Puccinia dioscorea*
- **Leaf spot:** *Cercospora dioscorea*
- **Leaf blight:** *Colletotrichum gloeosporioides*
- **Tuber rot:** *Fusarium* sp. and *Rhizoctonia* sp.

DATURA

- **Leaf spot -** *Alternaria tenuissima*
- **Root-rot:** *Sclerotium rolfsii*
- **Mosaic:** *Datura metel* mosaic virus

FRENCH BASIL

- ***Fusarium*** **wilt:** *Fusarium oxysporum* f.sp. *basilicum*
- **Damping-off:** *Pythium aphanidermatum*
- ***Botrytis*** **blight:** *Botrytis cinerea*

GLORY LILY

- **Bacterial blight:** *Pseudomonas syringae* pv. *syringae*
- **Leaf blight:** *Alternaria* sp.
- **Wilt:** *Fusarium* spp

GYMNEMA

- **Leaf blight:** *Colletotrichum dematium*
- **Powdery mildew:** *Erysiphe* sp.

GINSENG

- **Anthracnose:** *Colletotrichum dematium*
- **Powdery mildew:** *Erysiphe panax*
- **Leaf blight:** *Altenaria panax*
- **Damping - off:** *Pythium* sp., *Rhizoctonia solani* and *Phytophthora* sp.
- **Black root rot:** *Sclerotinia panacis*

HYOSCYAMUS

- **Leaf spot:** *Ascochyta kashmiriana*

- **Leaf blight:** *Alternaria alternata*
- **Seedling blight:** *Pythium butleri*
- **Bacterial blight:** *Pseudomonas cichorii*
- **Green mosaic:** *Cucumber mosaic virus*

INDIAN ALOE

- **Dry rot:** *Alternaria alternata*

ISABGOL

- **Downy mildew:** *Peronospora plantaginis*
- **Leaf blight:** *Alternaria* sp.
- **Little leaf:** MLO

LIQUORICE

- **Leaf spot:** *Cercospora cavarae*
- **Root rot, Collar rot and Wilt:** *Fusarium* spp., *Sclerotium* spp. and *Rhizoctonia bataticola*
- **Leaf blight:** *Phyllostictina glycyrrhizae*

BLACK NIGHT SHADE

- **Yellow mosaic:** *Manathakkali yellow mosaic virus*

Phyllody: Phytoplasma like organism (PLO)

NEEM

- **Leaf spot and blight:** *Colletotrichum gloeosporioides*
- **Powdery mildew:** *Oidium azadirachta*
- **Damping-off:** *Pythium* sp.
- **Leaf web blight:** *Rhizoctonia* sp.

PERIWINKLE

- **Rot:** *Phytophthora* spp.
- **Anthracnose:** *Colletotrichum dematium*
- **Stem rot:** *Rhizopus stolonifer*
- **Leaf blight:** *Alternaria alternata*
- **Root and stem rot:** *Fusarium* spp.
- **Periwinkle mosaic:** *Periwinkle mosaic virus*

PLANTAGO

- **Downy mildew:** *Peronospora plantaginis*
- **Damping-off:** *Pythium butleri*
- **Wilt:** *Fusarium oxysporum*

- **Powdery mildew:** *Erysiphe cichoracearum*

PODOPHYLLUM

- **Rust:** *Puccinia podophylli*
- **Leaf blotch:** *Spetotinia pcdophyllina*

SARPAGANDHA

- **Wilt:** *Fusarium oxysporum* f. sp. *rauvolfii*
- **Powdery mildew:** *Leveillula taurica*
- **Leaf blight and Bud rot:** *Alternaria tenuis*
- **Leaf spots:** *Cercospora rauvolfiae*
- **Target-spot:** *Corynespora cassiicola*
- **Anthracnose:** *Colletotrichum gloeosporioides*
- **Phyllody:** MLO
- **Yellow vein mosaic:** *Rauvolfia yellow vein mosaic virus*

SAFED MUSLI

- **Leaf blight:** *Colletotrichum capsici*

- **Tuber rot:** *Fusarium solani*
- **SENNA**
- **Pod rot:** *Bipolaris australiensis*
- **Leaf blight:** *Alternaria alternata*

DISEASES OF AROMATIC PLANTS

AMBRETTE

- **Blight:** *Alternaria alternata*
- **Wilt:** *Fusarium solani*

CHILLI

- **Damping-off:** *Pythium aphanidermatum*
- **Fruit rot and die-back:** *Colletotrichum capsici*
- ***Cercospora* leaf spot:** *Cercospora capsici*
- **Chilli mosaic:** *Chilli mosaic virus*
- **Chilli leaf curl:** *Tobacco leaf curl virus*
- ***Fusarium* wilt:** *Fusarium solani*
- **Powdery mildew:** *Leveillula taurica*

- **Bacterial leaf spot:** *Xanthomonas vesicatoria*

CORIANDER

- **Stem gall:** *Protomyces macrosporus*
- **Powdery mildew:** *Erysiphe polygoni*
- **Wilt:** *Fusarium oxysporum* f.sp. *corianderii*

CUMIN

- **Wilt:** *Fusarium oxysporum* f.sp. *cumini*
- **Blight:** *Alternaria burnsii*
- **Powdery mildew:** *Erysiphe polygoni*

DAVANA

- **Damping-off:** *Pythium aphanidermatum*
- **Bacterial blight:** *Ralstonia solanacearum*
- **Root-knot nematode:** *Meloidogyne incognita* and *M. javanica*

EUCALYPTUS

- **Mycosphaerella leaf spot:** *Mycosphaerella marksii*
- **Phavophloeospora leaf spot:** *Phavophloeospora eucalypti*
- **Pink disease:** *Erythricium salmonicolor*
- **Bacterial wilt:** *Ralstonia solanacearum*
- **Powdery mildew:** *Erysiphe cichoracearum*
- **Web blight:** *Rhizoctonia solani*
- **Damping-off:** *Pythium* spp. *Phytophthora* spp.
- **Rust:** *Puccinia psidii*

FENUGREEK

- **Powdery mildew:** *Erysiphe polygoni*
- **Root rot:** *Rhizoctonia solani*
- **Leaf spot:** *Cercospora traversiana*
- **Downy mildew:** *Peronospora trifoliorum*

FENNEL

- **Leaf blight**: *Ramularia foeniculi*
- **Leaf spot:** *Cercosporidium punctum*
- ***Alternaria* blight:** *Alternaria tenuis*

GARLIC

- **Neck rot and bulb rot:** *Botrytis allii*
- **Leaf blight:** *Stemphylium vesicarium*
- **White rot:** *Sclerotium cepivorum*
- **Black mould:** *Aspergillus alliaceous*

GERANIUM

- **Bacterial leaf spot/bacterial stem rot/bacterial wilt:** *Xanthomonas campestris* pv. *pelargonii*
- **Leaf rust:** *Puccinia pelargonii-zonalis*
- ***Botrytis* blight:** *Botrytis cinerea*
- **Root rot:** *Pythium* sp. or *Rhizoctonia* sp.

GINGER

- **Rhizome rot/soft rot:** *Pythium aphanidermatum*
- **Yellows/wilt:** *Fusarium oxysporum*
- **Leaf spot:** *Colletotrichum zingiberis*
- **Storage rots:** *Fusarium oxysporum, Pythium deliense* and *P. myriotylum*
- ***Phyllosticta* leaf spot**: *Phyllosticta zingiberi*

LEMON GRASS

- **Rust:** *Puccinia nakanishikii*
- **Leaf spot (eye spot):** *Helminthosporium saccharii*
- **Grey blight:** *Pestalotiopsis magniferae*
- **Leaf spot:** *Curvularia andropogonia*
- ***Colletotrichum* leaf spot:** *Colletotrichum graminicola*
- **Leaf spot and clump rot:** *Fusarium equiseti*
- **Smut:** *Tolyposporium christensenni*

MINT

- **Powdery mildew:** *Erysiphe cichoracearum*
- **Stolon rot or decay:** *Rhizoctonia solani*
- **Collar rot:** *Sclerotium rolfsii*
- **Rust**: *Puccinia menthae*
- ***Verticillium* wilt:** *Verticillium dahliae*
- ***Septoria* leaf spot:***Septoria menthae*
- ***Ramularia* leaf spot:** *Ramularia menthicola*

PALMAROSA

- **Red leaf spot**: *Colletotrichum graminicola*
- **Smut**: *Tolyposporium christensenii*
- **Little leaf or Grassy shoot**: *Balansia sclerotia*

PATCHOULI

- **Wilt:** *Fusarium solani*
- **Leaf blight:** *Alternaria alternata*
- ***Sclerotium* rot:** *Sclerotium rolfsii*

PEPPER

- ***Phytophthora* foot rot:** *Phytophthora palmivora*
- **Slow decline or wilt:** *Fusarium solani* f.sp. *piperi*
- **Anthracnose/Pollu disease:** *Colletotrichum gloeosporioides*

TURMERIC

- **Rhizome rot:** *Pythium aphanidermatum*
- **Leaf blotch:** *Taphrina maculans*
- **Leaf spot:** *Colletotrichum capsici*
- **Leaf spot:** *Cercospora curcumae*
- **Leaf blight:** *Rhizoctonia solani*

LIST OF AGRICULTURAL RESEARCH INSTITUTES
UNDER ICAR

1) Central Island Agricultural Research Institute, Port Blair
2) Central Arid Zone Research Institute, Jodhpur
3) Central Avian Research Institute, Izatnagar

4) Central Inland Fisheries Research Institute, Barrackpore

5) Central Institute Brackishwater Aquaculture, Chennai

6) Central Institute for Research on Buffaloes, Hissar

7) Central Institute for Research on Goats, Makhdoom

8) Central Institute of Agricultural Engineering, Bhopal

9) Central Institute for Arid Horticulture, Bikaner

10) Central Institute of Cotton Research, Nagpur

11) Central Institute of Fisheries Technology, Cochin

12) Central Institute of Freshwater Aquaculture, Bhubneshwar

13) Central Institute of Research on Cotton Technology, Mumbai

14) Central Institute of Sub Tropical Horticulture, Lucknow

15) Central Institute of Temperate Horticulture, Srinagar

16) Central Institute on Post harvest Engineering and Technology, Ludhiana

17) Central Marine Fisheries Research Institute, Kochi

18) Central Plantation Crops Research Institute, Kasargod

19) Central Potato Research Institute, Shimla

20) Central Research Institute for Jute and Allied Fibres, Barrackpore

21) Central Research Institute of Dryland Agriculture, Hyderabad

22) National Rice Research Institute, Cuttack

23) Central Sheep and Wool Research Institute, Avikanagar, Rajasthan

24) Indian Institute of Soil and Water Conservation, Dehradun

25) Central Soil Salinity Research Institute, Karnal

26) Central Tobacco Research Institute, Rajahmundry

27) Central Tuber Crops Research Institute, Trivandrum

28) ICAR Research Complex for Eastern Region, Patna

29) ICAR Research Complex for NEH Region, Barapani

30) Central Coastal Agricultural Research Institute, Ela, Old Goa, Goa

31) Indian Agricultural Statistics Research Institute, New Delhi

32) Indian Grassland and Fodder Research Institute, Jhansi

33) Indian Institute of Agricultural Biotechnology, Ranchi

34) Indian Institute of Horticultural Research, Bengaluru

35) Indian Institute of Natural Resins and Gums, Ranchi

36) Indian Institute of Pulses Research, Kanpur

37) Indian Institute of Soil Sciences, Bhopal

38) Indian Institute of Spices Research, Calicut

39) Indian Institute of Sugarcane Research, Lucknow

40) Indian Institute of Vegetable Research, Varanasi

41) National Academy of Agricultural Research & Management, Hyderabad

42) National Institute of Biotic Stresses Management, Raipur

43) National Institue of Abiotic Stress Management, Malegaon, Maharashtra

44) National Institute of Animal Nutrition and Physiology, Bengaluru

45) National Institute of Research on Jute & Allied Fibre Technology, Kolkata

46) National Institute of Veterinary Epidemiology and Disease Informatics, Hebbal, Bengaluru

47) Sugarcane Breeding Institute, Coimbatore

48) Vivekananda ParvatiyaKrishiAnusandhanSansthan, Almora

49) Central Institute for Research on Cattle, Meerut, Uttar Pradesh

50) National Institute of High Security Animal Diseases, Bhopal

51) Indian Institute of Maize Research,New Delhi

52) Central Agroforestry Research Institute , Jhansi

53) National Institute of Agricultural Economics and Policy Research, New Delhi

54) Indian Institute of Wheat and Barley Research, Karnal

55) Indian Institute of Farming Systems Research, Modipuram

56) Indian Institute of Millets Research, Hyderabad

57) Indian Institute of Oilseeds Research, Hyderabad

58) Indian Institute of Oil Palm Research, Pedavegi, West Godawari

59) Indian Institute of Water Management, Bhubaneshwar

60) Indian Institute of Rice Research, Hyderabad

61) Central Institute for Women in Agriculture, Bhubaneshwar

62) Central Citrus Research Institute, Nagpur

63) Indian Institute of Seed Research, Mau

64) Indian Agricultural Research Institute, Hazariba, Jharkhand

Deemed Universities

1) IARI- Indian Agriculture Research Institute – (Pusa, New Delhi)

2) IVRI-Indian Veterinary Research Institute- (Izatnagar, Utter Pradesh)

3) NDRI-National Dairy Research Institute (Karnal, Haryana)

4) CIFE- Central Institute for Fisheries Education (Mumbai, Maharastra)

CGIAR Consortium of International Agricultural Research Centers

1) **Africa Rice center** (ADRAO/WARDA), Cotonou, Benin.

2) **Bioversity International,** Maccarese, Roma, Italy

3) **International Center for Tropical Agriculture** (CIAT), Cali , Columbia

4) **Center for International Forestry Research** (CIFOR), Bogor, Indonesia

5) **International Maize and Wheat Improvement Center** (CIMMYT), Mexico , Mexico

6) **International Potato Center** (CIP), Lima , Peru

7) **International Center for Agricultural Research in the Dry Areas** (ICARDA), Aleppo, Syria

8) **International Crops Research Institute for the Semi-Arid Tropics** (ICRISAT), Patancheru, Telangana, India

9) **International Food Policy Research Institute** (IFPRI), Washington D.C., USA

10) **International Institute of Tropical Agriculture** (IITA), Ibadan, Nigéria

11) **International Livestock Research Institute** (ILRI), Nairobi , Kenya

12) **International Rice Research Institute** (IRRI), Los Baños, Philippines

13) **International Water Management Institute** (IWMI), Battaramulla , Sri Lanka

14) **World Agroforestry Centre,** Nairobi, Kenya

15) **WorldFish Center,** Penang, Malaysia